FROM YOUR CAPRICORN FRIEND

also by Henry Miller

FROM YOUR CAPRICORN FRIEND

Henry Miller and the *Stroker*, 1978–1980

Henry Miller

A NEW DIRECTIONS BOOK

Acknowledgements:
The letters and prose pieces first appeared in *Stroker* #7, the 1979 *Stroker Special* (chap book), *Strokers* #10, #11, #13, #17, and #19–25 published by Irving Stettner.

"An Open Letter to *Stroker!*" appears courtesy of Charlee Trantino.

"America, America" was written for Michel Waxman and André Cromphont as a foreword for a book of photographs to be published by Editions Complete, Brussels, Belgium.

Craig Peter Standish supplied Henry Miller's note to general correspondents.

Manufactured in the United States of America
First published clothbound and as New Directions Paperbook 568 in 1984
Published simultaneously in Canada by Penguin Books Canada Limited

Library of Congress Cataloging in Publication Data

Miller, Henry, 1891–1980
    From your Capricorn friend.

    Includes letters to Irving Stettner of Stroker magazine.
    1. Miller, Henry, 1891–1980—Correspondence.
2. Authors, American—20th century—Correspondence.
3. Stettner, Irving, 1922–   I. Stettner, Irving, 1922–
II. Title.
PS3525.I5454Z495   1984   818'.5209 [B]   83-17460
ISBN 0-8112-0890-7
ISBN 0-8112-0891-5 (pbk.)

New Directions Books are published for James Laughlin
by New Directions Publishing Corporation
80 Eighth Avenue, New York 10011

SECOND PRINTING

Publisher's Note

The Publisher wishes to extend appreciation and acknowledgment to two friends of Henry Miller: to Craig Peter Standish, who presented New Directions with the idea for this book and with his own copies of most of the material; to Irving Stettner for the title, the foreword, and assistance in assembling the book. And, a special salute to the "Prince of Second Avenue," Irving Stettner, for *Stroker* magazine itself, in which the letters and prose pieces here first appeared—to Henry Miller's and now a wider audience's delight.

CONTENTS

HENRYSAN AND THE *STROKER*
by Irving Stettner

First and last I regard Henry Miller as the best friend I ever had. Yes, sentimental, maudlin, half-cracked as it may sound. Alleluia, a-men!

How else can I feel toward a guy who would often write me in a letter, let drop: "Irv, can you use a bit of cash? I can always send you some. If so just let me know."

True, I was tempted to take him up on it once, twice. But never had the chance. Why? He just seemed to sense, uncannily, whenever I was broke; at such moments invariably arriving in the mail from him a substantial check; just a handout perhaps, but sent overtly as payment for copies of the latest *Stroker* to be dispatched to a whole slew of his friends, or he had decided to buy another one of my watercolors, etc.

In regard to friendship, perhaps it was like everything Henrysan did (his first name with the Japanese *san* suffix of affection added, how my pal Sava Nepus in Los Angeles and I always refer to him)—he went all the way. If you were his friend, there was nothing he wouldn't do for you; you were his brother, confidant, alter ego, Siamese twin, and if ever in a jam, off came the proverbial shirt off his back. All or nothing, yes. Just as years ago, in 1924 when Henrysan finally quit his job as personnel manager for New York Western Union, and decided to write; yes, he did just that, write, and nothing else—even if it meant going out to beg on the nearest street corner. But if you were his friend, he gave you more than money, far more; understanding, appreciation, and praise of your work (if it was merited, that is, since he was un-flinchingly—times even brutally—frank), big encouragement, and a plug anywhere down the line he could.

As for the two and half years in which he contributed to *Stroker*, early 1978 on, sent in original manuscripts and with no more than a little modest note "Irv, this is for *Stroker*, if you like," (*sic*, as if there was ever a question of sending a rejection slip to *Henry Miller*)—all I know is that it was the most thrilling, enraptured period of my life.

Each day was like a loaded six-shooter, packed full of surprises. I never knew what would arrive in the morning mail, what next from him: a long letter, a few words on a postcard, or another original manuscript; one of his books, new or old, but all with a warm dedication (he sent me over twenty); an original Henry Miller lithograph, numbered and signed, some six or seven; a handsome, deluxe first edition art book on Kandinsky, or a new biography out on Hermann Hesse; a Surrealist ink drawing of Man Ray disguised as Ferdinand Magellan, or, originally a present from his Chinese actress friend Lisa Lu, an Oriental funeral talisman i.e., a little woodcut of three enigmatic figures (Buddha disciples?) in bright magenta and gold ornately printed on fine rice paper. And other miscellaneous items among which was a request for the date of my birth, its place and exact time, so that he could have my horoscope done by a woman astrologer in the deep South (P.S. Two months later when my birthday rolled around, November 7th, there it was in the mailbox—a $150 check).

Mirabile dictu, yes. He even sent me a few of his friends. On a brief visit to New York, or passing through—in-between planes, so to speak—they would look me up, taxi down from Uptown. There was a young industrial designer from Detroit, a middle-aged professor from a New England college (though a lively one, I admit, a disciple of Orpheus), and a tall, voluptuous French brunette dressed exquisitely, chicly *à la Parisienne*, who worked for *Le Monde* . . . all come to knock on the door of my crumby one-room pad on lower Second Avenue! And perhaps some who never made it, those without the guts to walk past the flock of drunks, beggars, drug addicts, and overflowing garbage cans which adorn my front sidewalk. . . . One particular visitor I'll never forget: Christine Nazareth, a young, attractive, vivacious movie director from Rio de Janiero. She arrived like a gelignite bomb exploding, talking a mile a minute, bubbling over with laughter and waving her arms like an ecstatic octopus. And when I saw the car she had parked outside on the curb: a shiny black Rolls-Royce with a uniformed chauffeur no less which she had borrowed from her movie magnate producer . . . I almost flipped. In two seconds flat she had the chauffeur swinging open the door for me, I was piled into the back seat, and we were driving off to the nearest swank bar for an evening cocktail. "Yes, this is how it should be—nothing too good for the Prince of Lower 2nd Avenue!" she chortled, repeating Henrysan's words, the flattering sobriquet he had dubbed me with in his first *Open Letter* to Stroker.

Yes, he bowled me over with his gifts. He was generosity *per se*, magnanimous as a king, a god bestowing blessings. By way of expressing my gratitude, now and then I would send him a little watercolor. In due time they accumulated, he must have had a whole pile of them, since one day he wrote: "Thanks for the new watercolor. Gad, soon I'll have to start a Stettner gallery here!" At one point he was even seriously thinking of doing it: "am getting several of yours framed for a guest room," he wrote, "the Stettner museum or gallery." Yes, Henrysan, bless him, he really knew how to make a fellow feel good!

Even more than his gifts, what I relished most were his letters. Short or long, just one would have me floating on air for a week. Merely to open one was like uncorking a bottle of champagne, and one of rare old precious vintage at that. They simply sparkled, effervesced warmth, *camaraderie*, zest for life, enthusiasm for a certain writer or painter, steak dinner, particular person, etc. Not to speak of his self-mockery, his down-to-earth, pungent humor: "Irv, I am so overwhelmed with correspondence and interviews," he once wrote, "I don't know my ass from my elbow . . . Better to be a failure than a success! etc." And always so natural, frank, unpretentious, humble—half the time I wasn't sure who the hell was writing who: Gad, it seemed as if *he* was the novice writer and artist—and *I* was Henry Miller, the greatest writer of the 20th century! And so human those letters, so damn, deeply totally *human*. Putting one down after reading it, I confess it was often with a big lump in my throat, my eyes brimming over.

But what topped everything was what he would write at the end of almost every letter, or simply attach the names and addresses of a few of his hot fans. He was passing them on to me, so I could turn around and mail them printed flyers which included subscription blanks for *Stroker*. Yes, that took the cake. Since those names and addresses would number anywhere from a few to a dozen, two dozen, and one day even arriving from him a four page list of them in longhand, which Henrysan avowed, he took two afternoons off to write. A list which consisted of some sixty-five names! And all this at the tender age of eighty-seven.

In a few months the number of the mag's subscribers soared from thirty-five to one hundred and fifty. Not only that, but a lot of them hailed from England, France, Italy, Germany, Austria, Denmark, New Zealand, and so on. All of which I found thrilling, needless to say, like when I found myself corresponding with such a lyrical addressee as "Jean O'Brien, 10 St. Kevins Gardens, Dartry, Dublin, Ireland." But more so Henrysan, *de facto*, as it inspired him to think up a new slogan for the mag: "From the Ghetto to the Four Corners of the Earth," which has been used, proudly printed in every issue since.

So the *Stroker* for both of us, now you have the general idea: it was always a hell of a lot of fun, if nothing else.

"*Stroker?*"—what in hell does it mean: fish, fowl, vitamin pill, or American Jack the Ripper? You may have been wondering. Truth is, back in the summer of 1974 when I was putting together the first issue, and racking my brains for a name for the mag a whole solid week, it suddenly came to me quite by accident.

One afternoon I happened to walk into the Grassroots Bar on St. Marks Place. It was practically deserted; with only a couple of customers, and one was Rus Mayers. He was standing at the bar downing a boilermaker, sporting a brand new purple indigo shiner, and an idiotic grin.

Rus is a scaffold painter who in his spare time writes free verse love poems. He is a big, broad-shouldered hunk of a man, 6′ 3″, with hands like hams, but underneath gentle as a gazelle. He speaks softly, and has a hearty infectious laugh. I don't mind having a drink with him now and then; he knows some unique raunchy jokes, and can rap interestingly about William Carlos Williams, Hemingway, Sherwood Anderson, etc. Still, I try and stay clear of Rus. He drinks like a fish, and one drink too many—he's unpredictable, will act on sheer impulse. In fact, in a split-second he can be a raving madman.

Like any minute he is liable to jump up onto the bar, perhaps imagining it's a scaffold, and start dancing wildly, knocking over all the bottles and glasses. When I walked in that afternoon he was telling bartender Paul how he had picked up his black eye: "Know that Polish meat market on 1st Avenue?" Rus was saying in his soft, twangy Midwestern accent. "Well, a half hour ago I walked in there to buy a chicken, a whole one. I felt like cooking. You know Malik, the owner—that tall guy with a red-beet face? 'Sure, Rus, have some healthy fat hens in,' he says, 'just look 'em over.' Well, I turn around and there was his wife, a chubby buxom redhead standing in a corner, and smiling at me . . . Heck, I don't know what came over me . . . But I just walks up to her, reach out a hand and start feeling her big boobies . . . Heck, I don't know what Malik got so sore about—I only caressed them lightly . . . Anyhow: 'Hey, here's one with a great breast!' I said, 'how much?' Hell, I only meant it as a joke."

Meanwhile I'm at the far end of the bar—giving Rus plenty of elbowroom, naturally. But in a few seconds he spots me, and since Rus knows I spend a lot of time at the typewriter, I'm into being a poet, writer, he suddenly cries out cheerily: "Well, if it isn't the stroker!"

Implying by it, of course, someone who strokes with a pen.

Stroker . . . A word with a strong, resonant ring . . . It reechoed in my ears; yes, why not? Presto! I had the name for the mag.

What did Henrysan see in the *Stroker*, why did he like it so much? Question mark . . . Maybe it's the way I put an issue together; every few weeks or so, reading all the contributions which have come in the mail, this is what happens: if one rings a bell with me, a good clear, loud bell, without a second's hesitation, critical analysis, etc.—Socko! in it goes into the folds of the next issue. In other words I use pure and simply spontaneity. Regardless if it's a poem from a university professor, truck driver, dipsomaniac, or prisoner (come to think of it the best poems I ever printed *were* from prisoners). Also I'll print anything which happens to catch my eye—or pop it—in day-to-day living; a good letter arriving in the mail, a passage or two from an amazing book I may be reading, or even a piece of propaganda handed out to me in the street.

Perhaps Henrysan was attracted by—he even remarked on it once—a strong streak of Dada in *Stroker*. Why not? All told I've made three trips to Paris, lived there six years, so some of it must have rubbed off (besides some wackin' good meals, wines, wild hot love affairs, two cases of *chaudepisse*, and other sundry amazing experiences). Dada . . . if you're over twenty-six and don't know what it is, you should be ashamed of yourself. How to explain it? The best way might be to bring in the great German Dada poet Kurt Schwitters. Yes, and quote his famous line, "Blue is the color of my Love's yellow hair." Gad, what a line! (*Vive Kurt Schwitters!*) Or perhaps my own definition: Dada—"An insane lyrical impulse to remain light and carefree, always looking for something to wonder or marvel at, or love, or laugh at, but always remaining illogical and joyous in a world gone mad with too much logic, seriousness, science, newspapers, war, and destruction."

Sure, I'm editor of the mag. But I could be modest and say I have nothing to do with it; if it has any intrinsic qualities, it's all due to its contributors. Yes, thanks to them and in particular to Tommy Trantino, Seymour Krim, and Mohammed Mrabet (and his translator Paul Bowles), all of whom have faithfully sent in pieces to the last fourteen issues, each and every one. Yes, the mag's unsung heroes. And without them ever receiving—or even asking for—any payment, no, not a red cent. For doing same they were pure idiots, you might say, hell with being Dadaists. And you'd probably be right; but you'd also have to include yours truly in that category, since I also haven't made a dime out of the mag, so help me. I'm as poor as when it first started—if not *poorer*. Hell with it: I've printed my own writing in *Stroker* now and then. Yes, I've had my say. Or song, sonata or two, and even a few angry howls. Yes, I've had the last word a few times, and maybe a few last laughs. In any case I got it all off my chest, and sleep a hell of a lot better for it nights, period.

Or I could be vain and immodest and say *Stroker* owes everything to my own little crazy vision as to what a mag should be like. I could even paraphrase the famous repartee of Gustave Flaubert, who when asked to reveal the secret of his great masterpiece *Madame Bovary*, simply replied: "*Madame Bovary c'est moi!*" Likewise I could say: "*Le Stroker c'est moi!*"

When you get down to it, the contributors or yours truly, it's probably a combination of both.

Let's also be aware that Henrysan had a strong affection for the neighborhood from which *Stroker* springs, this Lower East Side, New York City. Did he romanticize it a bit? This jungle of overcrowded, decrepit, dank, airless, vermin-infested tenement buildings, these streets—East Houston, East Second Street, Allen Street, those down near Avenue B and Avenue C, etc.—streets like huge gashes in the flesh, open blood-clotted wounds, others sprawled out like gutted cracked fissures on the moon . . . But don't forget Second Avenue. Nor the host of immigrant Poles, Ukrainians, and Jews living here, its strong, down-to-earth East European flavor. And in Henrysan's day even more pronounced, as flourish-

ing then the great Yiddish theatre, a bevy of Russian and Rou-
manian restaurants, foreign cafes, and the Cafe Royale which was
frequented by the music critic James Gibbon Huneker, Israel and
Isaac Bashevis Singer, actors Boris Thomashefsky and Jacob Adler,
Molly Picon and others. Up on Fourteenth Street was the Labor
Temple where John Cowper Powys used to lecture. Yes, prowling
these streets in his youth, full of inchoate hungers, self-doubts,
frustrations, Miller must have found here a strong degree of com-
fort. As I myself actually feel here, even today. Walking on Second
Avenue particularly; for me it still emanates an intangible but dis-
tinct verve, splash of color, a certain European mellowness, human-
ness, a skipped heartbeat somewhere between tears and laughter . . . A magical aura, yes; perhaps left by all the writers, actors,
poets, and clowns who ever walked these streets? Who knows, but
all you need is a walk at twilight and sharp antennas out—and
angels are always flying over Second Avenue.

Henrysan also had a warm feeling for the many immigrants
here: the mass of underprivileged and poor, their humility to accept suffering—and hence experience joy. Yes, he was well aware
that in a world enslaved by money and machines, the only true
smiles left would have to come from "the foot of the ladder" (re:
The Smile at the Foot of the Ladder by Henry Miller). Keenly,
voraciously, ferociously as he was in touch with life, its beating
pulse and quick nerves, he well understood its deep underlying
paradoxes. Or the value of a single paradox, its fructifying qualities. As he once wrote me: "You are lucky living in that shit pile—
brings out the poet in you." And again, when he wrote in regard
to my editorship: "You are on the right track. (Second Ave.
Patrol). From that Ghetto you can reach the world far better than
a Madison Avenue address, believe me. Madison Ave. and Park
Ave. have an ominous ring to me. One spells chicanery; the other,
luxurious waste. *Ennahow* [sic] . . ." Also let's remember Miller's
deep insight into the whole American scene: he was well aware
that the rest of it, by and large, with its frenetic impulse to wor-

ship a heap of shallow, automated comforts and a dollar-geared, tenuous, sterile status quo—that was the real Ghetto, a spiritual one.

What it really all amounts to is simply another amazing episode in the fabulous, legendary life of Henry Miller: the boy from a lower middle class Brooklyn neighborhood who left job, family, and country to starve in the streets of Paris, sleep in doorways, and meanwhile jot down notes on scraps of paper which eventually would go into the writing of *Tropic of Cancer*, a book which in a few years would explode the whole Anglo-Saxon literary scene, and the European one too; then on to writing more books, some thirty or so, till he was finally recognized as one of the most important writer of modern times.

After all, has there ever been a precedent for it in all literary annals? I doubt it. As Irving Marder wrote in the *Los Angeles Herald Examiner*, August 5, 1979, in an article describing his unsuccessful attempts to obtain an interview with Henrysan: "*I was staggered. Not many writers would turn down the opportunity of an interview in the* New York Times Book Review. '*Dear Friend,*' *he* [Miller] *wrote, 'Sorry, but I don't want to do any biz with the N.Y. Times either. Consider it a funeral sheet—greatly overrated.' I wrote him again: what organ would he regard suitable for an interview?* Rolling Stone, Vogue . . . *or perhaps he would care to suggest one? The reply came on the back of another postcard-print of a Miller painting . . . 'Dear Friend,' he wrote. 'Sorry but I am still not ready to be interviewed. As for mags, the only one I write for is* Stroker, 129 2nd Ave. #3, New York, N.Y. 10003 . . .*"*

Yes, never before in history: here is a writer of world acclaim who elects to write exclusively—and gratis, needless to say—for one of the most obscure, little mags around! No wonder, often as I've related this and the above to a number of people, their reaction has been one and the same: they all shake their head dumbfounded, incredulous. As my Austrian friend Fred Peloschek remarks: "It would never, never happen in Europe. There, soon as a writer is well-known, he is printed only in the established reviews. But—" he adds, with a serene smile, "it's to be expected; who else would do such a thing . . . but Henry Miller!"

Ironically enough, as I write these words the *Stroker* is still not on its feet financially. For the past six issues—and we're now going into no. twenty-six—I've taken the layout to the printer with nothing but a fervent prayer on my lips. Yes, never sure how I was going to pay the bill . . .

Yet believe it or not, somehow the money has always turned up. At the last minute, a miracle, yes. One or a couple of subscribers— usually hot fans of Henrysan (William Giessel, Andrew Makowsky, Pamela Dewey, Allen Berlinski, et al.)—send in a generous donation; or quite unexpectedly, out of the blue, someone comes around and buys a few of my watercolors. Miracles . . . I'm actually beginning to believe in them. Or who knows, I already *do*.

Also it may have something to do with the last letter Henrysan wrote me, a couple months before he left us for Devachan. In a broken scrawl, since his eyesight was fading fast, one of the very last lines of the letter: "You and *Stroker* will always have it together."

But there is another few words he once wrote me, which I know I'll never forget . . . It was a few months after his work first appeared in the mag. Although requests for copies were beginning to come in from all over the world, it still wasn't enough, the printing bill still loomed large. However, now and then passing through New York, one of the new subscribers would pay me a visit. Every two weeks or so an unexpected knock on my door, and a strange face, bright-eyed, warm, smiling . . . There was Bob Volckens from Chicago, a young artist and smart as a whip whom I correspond with to this very day. And Diana Findley from Roanoke, Virginia, a blue-eyed blonde poetess who walked in with a big bundle of groceries and a bottle of rare Burgundy . . . Hell, I was making friends, if nothing else. So one morning thereabouts writing a letter to Henrysan, I remarked: "A new subscription came in the mail yesterday. Well, a new subscriber—a new friend."

A week later I had his reply, back of one of his painting postcards: "Irv, yes, 'making friends' *is* the main idea."

Irving Stettner

FROM YOUR CAPRICORN FRIEND

TO IRVING STETTNER
AND HIS *STROKER*

Pacific Palisades, Calif.
3/12/78

Bon jour, cher maître, et merci mille fois pour la troisième aquarelle!

Dear Irving—

You are more than generous, you are a Prince! The Prince of lower Second Avenue! *Banzai!*

For days and nights now I have been writing you in my head. The poem you wrote to me, plus the (two) wonderful water colors have had me in a dither. Also, the little fact that you apparently had not known Seurat's work. (For which you are readily forgiven. We can't know every fucking son of a bitch who puts brush to canvas.) Enough to know Hokusai, Bonnard, and a few others. Picasso we can forget—and Dali!

Anyway, what I am coming to is—*you*, you the artist (poet & painter). (Not Poet and Peasant, b'Jesus!) Yes, I have examined these W.C.'s in all conditions of light and weather. They remain *mysterious* to me. Which is what seldom happens with the celebrated ones! An exception is Van Eyck's *The Mystic Lamb* in the cathedral at Ghent. That still holds me spellbound *de loin*. Much as the actor with the cap in *The Dybbuk*.

What I call the *blue* W.C. turns out to be, like Joseph's coat, a thing of many colors. What is wonderful in these paintings, particularly if deliberate, is the use of tiny white spaces—like manna from above. Or like the perception of seemingly tiny details seen from the top of the Empire State Bldg. (is it still standing?).

Yes, those judicious "pauses," so to speak, combined with the massive inlay of many colors, creates not only an aura of mystery, but of perfection.

So your friend dubbed you another Francois Villon! (Do you know these lines attributed to him?

"Folle à la messe,

Molle à la fesse."[1]

Translated into English they have the same rhyme and same whatever.)

I am trying to recall where and when we first met. Why do I associate you both with Paris and Borough Hall, B'klyn?

I take it for granted that you, like myself, never learned to draw, never got to the Academy! (I used to be asked to leave the room when the Art class began—because I was *hopeless*.) Next month there will be an exhibition of thirty or more of my W.C.'s in Tel Aviv, Israel. It will be Kosher too. (And That's why I send you (now) only post cards of my work.)

Think of it—when I lived in Beverly Glen, Ca. I made W.C.'s for whomever for whatever they cared to send me. Now my (asking) price for a painting is $2000.00. I can't believe it myself. To tell you the truth, I would be happier giving them away, but as my royalties for books *decrease* I have to resort to these shenanigans to survive.

Today I signed two of my latest books for the King of Nepal. That gave me a lift. That I should be read in Nepal, if not in Weehawken, Hoboken, and Maspeth, L.I.

Did you receive a post card about Isaac and Moishe Pippik—the latter going nowhere (*nulle part*)?

I would like to do more in that vein, a sort of Woody Allen vein, if I might presume to call it that. But, as my ability to draw gets worse and worse I fall back on abstract fantasies where color compensates for lack of knowledge. Yet, child-like though these may seem, there is more of Kandinsky and Gogol in them than meets the eye.

[1] *"Frantic at Mass,*

Soft in the ass."

   Translated by Irving Stettner

Irving, I hope my writing is legible—I myself can barely decipher my own words.

Anyway, *Second Avenue*. In a far-fetched way it corresponds to my favorite Paris street—the rue Mouffetard, which takes off from the Place Contrescarpe where Hemingway is reputed to have lived. Yes, I will never forget Second Avenue—trying to sell boxes of imported candies at the Café Royal. Always thinking as I entered the cafe that here is where James Gibbon Huneker (music critic) used to read the newspaper over a cup of black coffee. And then the Houston St. Burlesk! A life saver to me in my days of migraine and neurosis! Always leaving the joint in good humor and fully recovered. (Shades of Margie Pemetti)

This was supposed to be for you and about you, my dear Irving. But you get mixed up with memories of places, people, events. You have a universal spirit. Instead of *Stroker* you should have named it "Joker." More fitting for its Dada background. Thank God you didn't take your stance from the Surrealists.

I try in vain to place you. At best, I make you out to be a Brooklyn boy, which is as good a moniker as one can invent for oneself. Strange, how crummy old Brooklyn (Williamsburg, Greenpoint especially) linger in one's mind and warm the gizzard. No matter how shitty it was or is, it had something. That *"je ne sais quoi"* that you like to use. I still speak with a Brooklynese accent, despite my fluent French and rudimentary German. (I would give a lot to have known Yiddish. I think it's a wonderful language for writers as well as comedians—what say?)

This is the longest letter I have written in a long time—even when I had two good eyes. Now I feel like a horse with blinders.

Irving, let me close by saying à la Lermontov that you are a hero of our time. One day I expect you to write a beautiful poem inspired by Sologub's *Gob of Spit*. You can take anything for your subject and make it come out like Chinese noodles. More power to you, old friend, and a million thanks for your gifts and your remembrances.

Keep on painting and writing. They will hear of you in Kathmandu before they do in L.A. or Buxtehude. No matter. Fuck 'em all!

Henry

Dear Irving—

Just a line to thank you for sending me (thru Charlee) that Trantino book.[1] It's out of this world! (I am only about half-way thru as I read very slowly now.) I wrote Charlee and thanked her. After I finish reading it Tony would like to read it, OK?

Also received that book of poems[2] you sent. Haven't read any yet but admired the black and white illustrations.

In a few days I hope to send you the catalog of my W.C.'s put out by The Coast Gallery in Big Sur. Exhibition in Tel Aviv[3] begins April 14th. Hope no terrorists invade the place.

That's all for now. I can see how you've become "The King of Second Ave." Good luck! Keep writing & painting—the only salvation in a cheesy world!

Henry

---

[1] *Lock the Lock* by Tommy Trantino.
[2] *On the 2nd Avenue Patrol* by Irving Stettner, illustrated by Pierre Jacquemon.
[3] Note: On a postcard sent later Henry Miller wrote; "Dear Irving, Just got word that I won first prize in Tel Aviv International Art Show. But no sales of paintings—Israelis too poor. Anyway, I wept."

Dear Irving, cher confrère,

Yesterday came another of your "no words for it" water colors and ink painting. Another beauty. Everyone who comes to the house loves it. And asks "Who *is* this guy who sends you all these beautiful gifts?"

And I say "An old friend from Brooklyn days. He runs a little mag called *Stroker*."

"Why *Stroker*," is the inevitable response.

"Haven't the faintest idea," I tell them.

Irving, today is not one of my good days. Seem to be all in and don't know why (the menopause probably). Or simply "le cafard." Irv, you say "ne fais pas." Shouldn't it be "ne *t'en* fais pas?" (Excuse me for mentioning it.) Anyway, that's what I'm doing anyway. Just pay it no never mind. *Merci mille fois!*

By the way, I don't want that little French book[1] done into English. No point to it. Get me?

Cheers any how!
Henry

---

[1] *Je Suis Pas Plus Con qu' un Autre*

AN OPEN LETTER TO STROKER!

Whoever would have thought that the venerable Alfred Knopf & Co. would have the courage and the foresight to publish Tommy Trantino's *Lock the Lock*.[1] *Hosanna!!! Salut!!! Merci mille fois! Banzai!* This marvelous book of the century could just as well have been taken for a lump of shit, *horse shit* what I mean. And it is a huge, a gargantuan piece of shit coming straight from a genius, from his mouth and from his ass-hole. It is the embalmed shit of the last days of Western civilization. *This is it—und nichts mehr!* This takes Homer, Dante, Goethe, and Fra Angelico to the dawn of a new world, something not to be called by that shitty name *Civilization!!!* This is Dostoievsky writing our death knell in the lingo of a junkie. I thought with Ernst Toller's *Broken Brow* I had tasted the last fart of our extinguished *Kultur*. Always, no matter what the weather, I tried never to forget Spengler's *Decline of the West* written during the first World War. How was I then (1918) to know there would be another and another and another—and then *whoosh. Sis, boom Ah!* the whole planet would explode. And why? As a result of civilized man's intellect. As a reward for his perseverance in the art of destruction.

But now, by some inexplicable mystery, Tommy Trantino has given us the works—from A to TZZIT. He has put it all in one book replete with maniacal illustrations as a handbook to Eternity. No, the human race will not be entirely destroyed—only us, us rats, roaches, lice, weasels, know-it-alls. A new race is in the offing. Maybe not exactly a "human" race, but a race of beings who know how *not* to *kill, not* to *murder, not* to *assassinate, rape,* and *plunder.* And so unknown to most of mankind, the man of the hour is Tommy Trantino sitting in a cell for life somewhere in the wilds of New Jersey. He wasn't what you would call an angel or a saint. Far from it. He was the spawn of our sick society. He made his

[1] *Lock the Lock* by Tommy Trantino. Ink-drawing illustrations by the Author. Alfred A. Knopf publishers 1974; Bantam Books edition, 1975.

debut by shitting in his pants. That was the first sin he committed. The others followed *sui generis*.

I don't believe he killed those two cops for which he is doing a long stretch. No, I don't believe any of the shit they trumped up to do away with him. With only this one book so far he has already given evidence of being the "sequel" to our beloved Dostoievsky. Certainly he talks a different language, certainly their styles are far apart. But there is a connection. The two of them possessed that rare thing called "a soul" (*and no holy water involved*). About the two cops who he was accused of killing in cold blood . . . From the ruckus they made over these deaths you'd think he (or some one) had killed two sacred bulls from the temple of Shiva.

When a cop is killed by a bullet, a knife, or a bomb it's a calamity. *But,* how many innocent victims have *they* put away in cold blood—and nary a tear!

No, it's far from being the greatest civilization that ever was. Nor are our famous intellects the greatest ever. For one thing, all their ingenuity seems to have gone into the making of instruments of destruction. Somewhere there is always an enemy—millions of enemies. They lurk not only in strange parts of the world but in our own bodies. (Those are the hardest to combat.)

When we investigate the treasures of lost civilizations we discover works of art far superior to our own. With them Art was a pastime. With us *killing* is the pastime and dope the inspiration. In our time, our civilization, to be an artist one must live in exile, the sport of society, for at least ten years. The chances are that, even though a genius, one can die in the gutter.

Trantino's wife, Charlee, writes me that after being in prison for fifteen years Tommy expects a parole two years from now. To a man who has spent that much time behind the bars two years can sound like 20,000 years.

I am writing these lines because of my friendship with Irving Stettner, the editor of that little magazine called *Stroker*. Irving is an old friend of mine and an artist in the true sense of the word.

It is through him that I came to know about Tommy Trantino. Irving visits him occasionally and always comes away exalted, uplifted. *Irving*, mind you, not Tommy. A very revealing, very significant fact. I now have three friends who are in for life. All three write me wonderful letters. One of them was on TV once with his warden. He (too) had allegedly killed a cop. But he was no "animal" or maniac. In fact, he would pass in the outside world for a wonderful human being. Not all inmates are wonderful beings, to be sure. But there are these exceptions and they deserve recognition. Often the real criminals go free after a brief term, especially political figures. I have only to mention Watergate and I am sure you will understand. For some of these birds it means a chance to earn some extra loot by writing their memoirs or whatever. Strange how the public will read such crap and allow the real stuff to go by unnoticed.

For some prisoners life gives them the opportunity to find spirited release—find Jesus, in other words. But would any one in his sane mind recommend a term in prison as a means of seeking spiritual bliss? Now and then a truly remarkable book gets written by a prisoner while in jail. Cervantes is one example. Marco Polo another. But these are what you might call "sublime accidents." Mostly the prisoner grows embittered, or hopeless, which is even worse.

I have often thought that a way to prevent judges from meting out harsh sentences would be to make them spend a term in prison before being made judges. A few months in solitary, for example, might go far toward softening them up. On further thought a term in solitary seems too soft. If I were to establish a course of training for a judge (and perhaps for criminal lawyers as well) I would certainly advocate in addition to occasional solitary confinement flogging once a month, being buggered at least once a week, bread and water diet weekly, no exercise, no fresh air, the lousiest food and the most inhuman living conditions imaginable. Dostoievsky not only survived similar treatment but he became an extraordinary judge of human nature and the greatest writer of modern times. Oh yes, I forgot to add that in addition to the above regimen I would oblige would-be judges to read Lao-tse, Chuang-tzu, Rabelais, and Dostoievsky's *The Idiot*.

In closing I pray that Tommy Trantino receive due recognition as an artist from the public. Bless his soul!

Dear Irv—

I was just glancing through the *On the Second Avenue Patrol: Selected Poems* you sent me a week or more ago—always behind, so much fucking mail each day . . . Anyway I stumbled on your "Song—Presidential Day"—and I recognized that at once as poetry—*the poem, quoi!* Yes, Irv, you certainly have something most of your colleagues *don't* have—ART—LIFE—JOY—SUN—STARS—LOVE. Seymour Krim's foreword is rather good but doesn't go far enuf. The French friend who dubbed you a modern François Villon comes closer to the truth. You're just a bundle of never-ending enthusiasm. I could read you all day—but not these other guys, not most of them anyway. And you have a wonderful flair for swiping wonderful bits from Cendrars and many others—bravo! You get away with murder.

I write these few lines before settling down to *work. Work!* You settle up to *sing.* That's what poetry is all about. Vive le poème! Vive Irving Stettner! Vive Tommy Trantino! Vive Second Avenue! Don't move, don't travel! Second Avenue is your daily inspiration. Nourish it with your poems & prose!

Henry

Dear Irving—

Your three letters arrived today. Wow! What enthusiasm, what appreciation! If only one could generate that in the public at large!

Irving, the idea of doing a chap book suits me fine, with one exception. I wouldn't like it to be in company with a gang of protesters. With T.T. O.K. But I never belonged to any movement, any cult or ism. At twenty-one I was an anarchist and have remained one all my life. (But more like Prince Kropotkin than the guy who shot the steel magnate.)

I agree too with your choice of the ink drawings, especially No. 9. Now let's see what T.T. thinks of it all. Maybe he'll be agin it!

Don't worry about your review of Mathieu. He's a great scholar but a real human being. He was here at my home for a week some months ago. A "dromomaniac" like Rimbaud and myself. Today I can't even go for a walk. And sight bothers me.

But a thousand thanks for your fantastic reception of the letter. More anon.

Henry

P.S. Do you know that Tommy's book is now in paper back—by Bantam? For $1.49 or something like that. Do you think I should send copy of letter to Knopf or/and the parole officer?

HM.

Dear Irving—

Thank you for the book of poems by your good friend Stephanie Miller. I have read most of her poems and now and then in *Stroker* too.

But Irving, I have a sad confession to make to you—about modern poets. (All except yourself—because you are also a *poet in life*.) I just don't get what modern poets are trying to say. Certainly Rimbaud or the other French poets did not spawn them. Rimbaud, at the end of his life—said to an old friend "Don't talk to me about that stuff (poetry). I'm thru with all that shit."

Rimbaud is more famous, I believe, for his prose poems, which I dig. Forgive me for being so blunt, Irving. But *poetry* is one of my weak points.

So you too have unrequited loves now and then?

By the way, my *Insomnia* can now be bought for $1.49 a copy (the $10.00 edition) from the Outlet Co., % Crown Publisher, N.Y.C. It's a beauty of a book, I think.

Henry

On my new letter heads I will print at bottom—"I piss on it all from a considerable height." L.-F. Céline

Ps. Hope all went well when you saw T.T. [Tommy Trantino]. Charlee sounds great. How lucky he is! What about sending parole officer & Knopf copies of the Chap Book? (*Je ne sais pas quoi*). Cheers!

Dear Irv—

So glad to know you are dispensing with Greenberg's[1] piece—
because T.T. (Tommy Trantino) did not want him! Bravo! Listen, I read (a few hours ago) that long love poem you designated
(in *Stroker*). Man, that really *is formidable!* You mention so many
names that trigger me off—one especially—*Swami Vivekananda*.
I have the greatest admiration for his writings—and since long,
long ago. Was utterly surprised to see *you* mention him. In any
case, that poem is just about everything under the sun. *Fabulous.*
No wonder the French woman called you a real poet—than which
there can be no greater compliment in French or any other language.

I want to write you yards of things but don't have the time.
Just back from my weekly visit to heart doctor. I am supposedly
suffering from angina pectoris. Today he says undoubtedly that is
it. I ask if my pains could be *psychosomatic.*—he shook his head
No. He's just a physician, no *mantic* personality. I think it's psychosomatic because I am in the throes of deep love and had a
doubting spell the other day (for wrong reason). Your writing does
wonders for me. Man, you have a heart—and great feeling. You
let "it" (whatever that may be) rule! Bravo! With you everything
is "autonomous"—not just stomach, liver, kidneys etc. Why
should head be exempt? Does head rule us—or— ?

You know, just as I can't abide your friend Allen Ginsberg so I
have no use for Jesus the Christ, Moses, Abraham, or the Buddha
hisself. I am probably a Zoroastrian—I believe good and evil are
two sides of same coin. Can't abide these all-good people!

I have to stop now.

My loved one just stopped by unexpectedly to say Hello to me.
That knocks my angina pectoris for a loop. I feel twenty-six not

---

[1] Erron., Ginsberg.

eighty-six. You write like Rimbaud—perpetual youth, perpetual adoration. Stick to it, Irving.

We're both Brooklyn boys, eh wot? I was from Driggs Avenue—now there are synagogues where there used to be Catholic churches.

Nuff said!

I understand about royalties on Chap Book.[2] Use the fifty I returned to pay the printer. Always give my best to Tommy.

Yes, had *wonderful* letter from him the other day. Bless Charlee too.

Henry

---

[2] "An Open Letter to Stroker!" by Henry Miller, *Stroker Chap Book* 1978.

Irving—

Forgot to answer about reprint of my letter in your friend's mag. Irving, I leave this to your discretion. Are you sure it won't interfere with sales of the Chap Book?

If you agree with me about Ginsberg's text (friend or no friend) do look again at the very last chapter of *Siddhartha*. What I refer to is where Siddhartha tries to explain to his old friend Govinda the secret of the art of living. He picks up a stone and starts talking. From there on you will see what I mean. And you'll also see the difference between Ginsberg and Hesse—or/and the *real* Buddha. Siddhartha meets the historical Buddha, if you remember, pays his respects to him but adds *"I have to find my own way. . ."* Hope I make myself clear.

Don't think I am returning check because it's too small. Coming from you and *Stroker* it's magnificent. Thank you again,

Henry

Dear Irv—

Salut! Merci pour tout. David Cohen did an excellent job—thank him for me.

I've already used up all the Chap Books you sent me—waiting for more. Figure I can use altogether about twenty-five—possibly more later—or, should it go into a second printing. (This one was a thousand, yes?)

Tommy sent me a wonderful letter and an unusual painting (don't know if W.C. or what—but unique.) This before receiving Chap Book.

I'm going to try to reach (via the book) publishers, lawyer friends, film people who just *may* be interested. All hazardous and dubious, of course. *Comme tu sais bien!*

Right now I am afflicted with "herpies zaster" or in common language the shingles. Very painful tho' not a dangerous ailment. To forget it I am writing me head off. Just corrected typescript of Vol. III, *Book of Friends*—don't know yet what title to give it as it is a mixture of ten women's portraits (short ones) and a long chapter on "Alf" (Perles). Every night I try to read a few pages more in the book on Cendrars. The exact title is *Blaise Cendrars—Discovery and Recreation*.[1] Published by University of Toronto Press in Toronto, London *and* Buffalo (sic). Every night I go to bed with my head swarming with names and places, authors, painters, *Dadaists,* etc. (*You* belong with the Dadaists!) You're a wonderful example of what Cendrars always talked about—the poet-in-life. When I first saw *Stroker* I never believed I would find such genes in it as I have. I suppose you read Apollinaire—his *Alcools* (poem)? Man, you will get itchy reading this book. I am only around page seventy having to read so slowly. But it's like getting injections of Vitamin B-12 magnified.

Are you sending copies, or offering copies to certain book stores

[1] Author is Jay Bochner

of Chap Books? I should think Gotham, N.Y., Westwood Book-shop, L.A., Papa Bach, L.A. would certainly be interested. Price is very cheap—only $1.50, isn't it?

Waiting to hear from Charlee if I should send copy to Parole officer, Dietz. And what about Knoff & Bantam? Will you take care of them or what? Must stop now—*je ne sais pas pourquoi*—your favorite expression. All the Best!

Henry

Dear Irving—

Today came (two) copies of Seymour Krim's book—one from you and one from him. Unfortunately my bad eyesight won't permit me to read it. But I'll write and thank him.

More important was your letter about Marie Corelli. That was most heartening to me, as most people to whom I've recommended her work just ignore her. The *Romance of Two Worlds* may have been her first book. A much better one is *The Sorrows of Satan*, which many years ago was made into a movie here in Hollywood. (Never saw it, but can't imagine it could have been good.) The one you're reading now—*The Life Everlasting*—is the best, in my opinion. Why don't you write about your experience in reading her in the next *Stroker*? I'd love to read what you have to say. But be sure to read *Sorrows of Satan* first!

And now—the most important—simply astounding—your best to date by a long shot: the water color you so kindly sent me. Irv, you caught the trick which George Grosz used—*damp paper*. Sandy had put it on the shelf in the dining room with your others. I came upon it accidentally. Couldn't believe it was yours. It's absolutely unique among all your works. Congratulations! *Muzzletoff!* Happy New Year (Rosh Hashannah). And yesterday our favorite, Isaac Singer, wins the Nobel Prize. What a wonderful succession of events. I am so busy—with chores—not painting— I can hardly turn around.

Yesterday Brenda and I had our pictures taken together by a Hollywood photog she models for some times. Today she saw the proofs and called to tell me they were *incredible*. We look like the "Eternal Lovers." Can you beat it?

Which reminds me—you never sent me a photo of your Anna. Do, please send me a print if you can.

Your visit still lingers in my memory. Everybody you met remembers you and that you were or are *the poet*, the genuine one.

That pleased me immensely. Sava always asks about you. Still working nights for me—as a hobby.

Well, Irv, they're calling me in for dinner. Bless you—Carry on in that new W.C. vein. *Fantastique*!!!

Henry

Dear Irving,

What memories those Brooklyn street names and districts evoke! I know *all* of them except Canarsie—never went there. But I lived near Bushwick Ave. on Decatur St. for ten years or so. My friends Tony and Joey[1] lived in Bensonhurst. (Do you remember Ulmer Park near there, where open air vaudeville was given—you sat at round tables and ordered beer, coffee, sandwiches. I heard Adeline *Patti* sing there!) All I need to know now is your birth date. I believe in astrology—in its "sychronicity," as Jung put it.

Sure, send Knopf & Bantam copies.[2] Maybe *shame* them!

Am mailing David Cohen two Chap Books tomorrow. Wrote him nice letter yesterday.

Today received fifteen copies of *Insomnia* to be autographed. Sent from a book store in Kosciusko, Miss.!!! Can you beat that?

Also mailing T.T. and Charlee copy of *Insomnia* tomorrow.

Yes, Tommy's poem good example of haiku. I wrote (two) poems recently which *you* inspired but sent them to my girl friend Brenda V*enus*—real name! Have the most wonderful harmonious and affectionate relationship with her. But don't spread the news around.

Must quit now. I remember eating in Polish restaurant near you *sixty* years ago. Immaculate and tasty.

How about a pastrami sandwich?

Cheers!

Henry Miller

---

[1] *Joey* by Henry Miller Capra Press 1979.
[2] "An Open Letter to Stroker!" *Stroker Chap Book* 1978.

Dear Irv (and his *Stroker!*),

More ink work from you today. Very "springy"—congratulations. By the way, would you want a set of those ink drawings I did for Tommy? I have (two) sets his brother printed. Do give him warm regards if this letter arrives in time.

Irv, I am spinning like a top here. No *2nd Ave. Patrol* but Ocampo Drive. (Do you recall that the South American poetess, Victoria Ocampo, was Keyserling's mistress?)

Now that I see the photo you sent I recognize how, what & where. It was sent to me from Bangkok by my Chinese actress friend Lisa Lu, who had finished work in a film for Bogdanovich done in Singapore. It was a piece of cloth, *non*? This reminds me—did I ever send you a copy of my little book in French called *Je Suis Pas Plus Con Qu'un Autre*? If not, I will pronto.

You send me so many things—I feel I am always on the receiving end.

In yesterday's issue of *People* mag there was an interview with yours truly. Lousy, I thought, by comparison with the answers I gave *viva voce*. The only good thing in it is the little photo of me kissing my friend Brenda Venus. It is not true that she comes several times a week to paint with me. It just happened that day that when interview ended she and I did a water color together. (Turned out damn well, in a Dada way, if you know what I mean.)

Then the next day we get a phone call from Gov. Brown asking if he can visit me. I said sure, of course, and he came with his chief aide (a Frenchman whose name I forget now—sounded more Russian than French—but a swell guy). Anyway, we gave them some white wine while they watched us eat dinner. He stayed two and a half hours. Talked frankly and vivaciously, and when he left asked if he could return soon again.

The next day comes a German woman and her husband from Munich. Brings me a book gotten up by some fans of mine. Had a few photos of ancient W.C.'s which was a nice surprise. But the Germans, even when they love you, are terrible bores. As I told Gov. Brown—"I think Billy Graham is an ass-hole"—he exploded with laughter. We talked of Zen and Siddartha and many things. You would have enjoyed it. He liked my water colors too—they happened to be spread out on the ping pong table.

Tonight comes a Dr. Roberts and his wife to cook dinner for me. Haven't seen them in twenty years. Am afraid they will bore the shit out of me.

Last night it was a film producer and director. I *annihilated* them! But they too asked if they could return for me. I must be getting to be a one man *Cirque Medrano*, what!

Well, thank you again for the pics! It's great to hear how you are selling. I wish you could latch on to that guy in Kosciusko, Miss.—he buys everything, it seems.

Imagine me becoming famous in Mississippi, rather than L.A., Chicago or New York!

Cheers!

Henry

P.S. Before I started on the "Nightmare" trip I met Sherwood Anderson (my then hero) in a hotel bar. I asked him what was his favorite spot in the U.S. He said—"Biloxi, Miss." (I too loved it.)

CUANDO MERDA TIVER VALOR POBRE NASCE SEM CU

This is on my front door to keep faces away.

"When a man has reached old age and has fulfilled his
mission, he has a right to confront the idea of death in
peace. He has no need of other men, he knows them already
and has seen enough of them. What he needs is peace. It
is not seemly to seek out such a man, plague him with
chatter, and make him suffer banalities. One should
pass by the door of his house as if no one lived there."

(Meng Tse)

Was originally on H. Hesse's own door!! HM

Dear Irv—

Your two poems came today—great. Especially the one translated—how all improves (even the shit!) in French, eh? I don't know why but suddenly I am reminded to tell you of Havelock Ellis' Introduction to *A Rebours* by Huysmans. ("Against the Grain." It's out in a sort of pocket edition). It should take some time to read but should set you dancing. No more writers like Havelock Ellis today. Or Cendrars, or Elie Faure, or even that unheard of Marie Correlli. When you have nothing better to do some day, look for her *The Life Everlasting*. Then you'll know the role of doubt in love!

Irv, that was smashing to sell all those aquarelles. Your answer to prostitute would never have come to my mind. "Beauty." *Wunderbar!* Shows what a poet you are.

Today Sandy is mailing you a colored photo (big size) of a water color I gave Brenda. One of my best—recent vintage. I wanted it for my self but then when I thought of all the gifts you bestowed on me I said "Fuck it! it belongs to Irv." One day I'll send you an original. That fucking Coast Gallery in Big Sur has only sold six or seven so far. (Asks too much—$2000 each! Wowie! Can buy a used car for that!)

I didn't know I had said anything humorous in my letter about Gov. Brown. Sometimes I say funny things when I'm in a dolorous state. (Not often!) Mostly I retain my moral and spiritual equilibrium. I miss Second Ave. . . . those peregrinations and the foreign cafés. Especially *The Royal*. You are lucky living in that shit pile—brings out the poet in you. Here it's a polished morgue—I mean the neighborhood, Pacific Palisades. I was far happier in the sordid streets of Paris—or even Brooklyn. Driggs Avenue (662) stands there, the house, like the only tooth left in a rotten jaw. (Did you notice the French actor—forget his name—died—com-

mitted suicide the other day? I was going to say "Raoul Dufy."
Shows you the cracks in my head. *Charles Boyer*.)

You know, that monicker "The Second Ave. Patrol" always re-
curs, like a melody. This morning, b'Jasus, I wake up trying to
remember a (Shakespeare verse) song we sang in Eastern District
High School—Barney O'Donnell at the piano, teaching us Irish
phrases in between, like "Faugh a balla!" ("Clear the way!") He
was a Sinn Feiner. Anyway, the song begins "Hark, hark! the lark
at heaven's gate sings, and Phoebus 'gins arise, his steeds to water
at those springs . . ." and then I'm lost. Do *you* recall that last
line? Funny, the things one wakes up with at eighty-seven years
of age. You might think CUNT—but no, for other things, past
and future. Reveries are better (for me) than meditation. Never
could meditate properly. Makes me think of Ginsberg and his
little music box—*and* plectrum.

Well, enuf for to day. You have "red letter" days every day, it
seems. Your ancestors must have come from the Jewish part of
Thibet!

Selah!

Henry

"HENRY, NOW AND THEN I MAY BE OBLIGED TO SLEEP IN MY CAR, BUT WHEN
I NEED TO TAKE A SHIT I GO TO THE BEVERLY HILLS HOTEL."
(*Florian Steiner*)

She was unquestionably a sexy bitch, one would say. And he, well he was like a guy without a pair of balls. An odd couple, truly. They had met on a transcontinental flight. Both were headed to the same place: Vienna. It seems that he had been born and grew up there; she had never been out of the U.S.A., but held romantic notions about all of Europe, particularly countries like Austria, Hungary, Romania, and Yugoslavia.

There was nothing in the least romantic about *him*, though he looked as if he could be. He was really down to earth, a most practical-minded son-of-a-bitch. Hard-boiled, one said of him.

She on the other hand was full of love and tenderness, sincere and unfortunately what we call a "loser." She seemed made to hold on to anyone she fell in love with, and she fell in love as often as she was ditched. In short, she was a fool for love, a prey to the wolves.

In deciding to visit Vienna of all places she hoped there to meet up with men who were *different*. Vienna itself she saw as a charming and beautiful Old World capital. She imagined that droshkies were still being used.

The two happened to have end seats across the aisle from one another. It began by him offering her a drop of brandy from his hip flask. She had ordered tea and lemon. Something about the way she refused his offer of a "little snifter" started the machinery going in him. That she was not the usual, ordinary type impressed him immediately. It awakened his slumbering sexual ardor. He decided he would try and make her.

"Ever been to Vienna before?" he queried. She shook her head by the way of answer. "Going to stay there for awhile?" he continued.

"I really don't know," she replied. "It depends."

"On what, may I ask?"

"Oh, lots of things," she answered. "By the way, have you ever been there?" With this his face lighted up. (Here was his chance.)

"Have I ever *been* there? Lady, I was *born* there. I know the place like a book."

It was her turn to suddenly become interested. (What a guide! she thought to herself.)

"Is it still as beautiful as ever?" was her next question.

To her astonishment he replied, "Yes and no. It depends on how you look at it."

She thought this a rather queer response and begged him to be more explicit.

"Well," says he in a drawling Brooklynese way, "Vienna is like a whore you once loved and has now grown old and slightly decrepit. Nevertheless she still retains a few patches of her former beauty" (becoming more daring) "—mostly in bed."

He wondered if perhaps this last phrase might terminate the conversation. To his surprise she rose to the bait like a fish.

"That's quite a poetic picture of Vienna you draw," she remarked. "You must feel much at home, greatly attached to your birthplace."

"On the contrary," he snapped. "You see, though I know the city well, I am not attached to it emotionally. To me it's just another city."

"That's rather peculiar, isn't it?" she ventured to say.

"You see I lost my mother when a boy—and I've never really gotten over it."

"That's queer," she rejoined. "I lost my mother too when a girl. But I no longer miss mine. That may explain why I fall in love so easily . . . Does that sound a little silly to you?"

"On the contrary," said he, "I understand perfectly." He took another nip from his flask. (She would fall right into the trap, he thought: going easier than he had expected.)

"Have you booked a hotel?" was his next question.

She hadn't but she thought she could find one easy enough. To this he remarked as casually as possible that his family had a little chateau right in the heart of the city. It had many unfilled rooms; she was welcome to stay there if she liked.

She thought this adorable of him. So kind, so sweet. She never suspected a thing. He was a gentleman from the Old World.

(The truth was, of course, that he came from a part of Brooklyn near the Gowanus Canal. But he spoke German rather fluently and had the natural ability of seeming to be at home anywhere.)

At the airport he commanded a horse-drawn cab, one of those old-fashioned kind which were so much more genteel than our taxis of today.

The "chateau" turned out not to be a chateau but what we would call a mansion today. He showed her about the place, pointing out rare *objets d'art*, etc. Finally she asked to be shown the sleeping quarters. At this point, oddly enough, she asked him for his name. "Albert," he said—"just Albert. And yours?" "I have a simple name too," she said. "It's Nellie. I didn't tell you but I hail from Shreveport, Louisiana. I'm a Southerner."

"You look like one, but you don't talk like one. You have no accent."

"That's because I was an actress for awhile. I had to lose my accent quickly."

Suddenly she broke into an old popular song: "Wait till the Sun Shines, Nellie":

And the clouds go drifting by, we will be happy, Nellie
Bye and bye . . . .

She sang it in a soft, contralto voice with just the touch of an accent.

"That was beautiful," he said. And then, abruptly, pointing to the bed, he blurted out: "And this is our bedroom. Do you like it?"

She thought it divine, naming some French period to which it belonged. Then, just as abruptly as he had pointed out "our" bed she asked: "Is there a douche bag in this house?"

He was taken aback, flabbergasted. For once it was all clear sailing. He never dreamed it would be this simple. He felt his prick getting stiff.

"Why a douche bag?" he demanded. "Don't you use the pill—or have you got the curse?"

"No, I can't use the pill—doesn't agree with me. Can't you trump up a good old douche bag?"

"I'll send for one at the pharmacy, don't worry." With this he began slowly and gently peeling off her clothes. She had a beautiful figure, especially her buttocks. He couldn't resist kissing them after she had removed her panties.

They jumped into bed, and for the first time in ages, he enjoyed a real, honest-to-god fuck. They lay awhile chatting about Shreveport and her life as a young cunt, when suddenly she cried, "Where's that douche bag? I don't aim to get pregnant right off the bat."

She coaxed him into the bathroom to help her. Seems that, to be sure it worked properly, she stood on her hands and had the man insert the hose deep in her cunt. That way she felt safe.

It turned out that she too enjoyed very much their first get-together. In the week that followed they did a lot of fucking—morning, noon, and night. She hadn't had much fucking for the last two or three years, ever since she split with the rich nabob who had been keeping her.

Between times they toured the city—cabarets, music halls, opera houses, fancy bars, and so on. And always in elegant style. He really did know his Vienna.

Then one afternoon, when they were to go to a concert, he told her he couldn't go. Asked why, he replied, "I have to appear in court."

"Are you in trouble?" she asked tenderly.

"Baby, you bet I am."

"But what did you do?"

"Nellie, I've got to set you straight," he found himself saying.

"I'm nothing but a crook—a high class crook. I handle phony stocks and bonds."

"And now they've caught up with you, is that it?"

"Not quite," he quickly replied. "I have some very able lawyers. But, you never know."

With this off his chest, he looked squarely at her, and to her surprise, he blurted out, "Nellie, I love you."

At that she broke down and began weeping—real tears, real sobs.

"Oh Albert," she murmured, "and I was just beginning to fall in love with you. You know, you never said a word about love. I thought you just loved my body. . . ."

He interrupted. "That's right. That's what I love about you—your ass, your cunt, your cute Southern ways."

"Didn't you feel just a wee bit of love for me?" she asked pathetically.

"Nellie," he said, "get things straight in your little head. Men don't fall in love so easily; it's cunt they're after. Plain, honest-to-goodness *cunt*. The juicier the better. All that love stuff is just a come-on. Don't you realize that?"

"I've suspected as much," she replied, "but I always hoped that if I loved someone dearly, he would love me back. I believe in love, not sex, though I'm not ashamed to enjoy a good fuck when it happens. What we women need, though, is not the stiff prick but love, someone who cares and cares deeply. I've fallen in love again and again. Luckily I never married. (I'm not that much of an idiot!) One day I *know* I will find the man who loves *me*. (I'm sure there is such a man.)"

"But Nellie, I just told you—*I love you!*"

She shook her head slowly and looking directly into his eyes, she said quietly, "No, Albert, you're not my man, you love cunt. You're cunt-happy. You don't know what love is. . . . Besides, I couldn't live with a crook, even a high class one. I'm grateful to you for showing me Vienna. As you said on the plane—'She's a bit like a decrepit whore but still retains some patches of beauty.' Yes, Albert, those little patches were worth more to me than all of Manhattan, Chicago, Boston, or Los Angeles. I will always be thankful for the things you taught me. You were just wonderful in bed. But we don't spend our whole life in bed, do we?"

For the first time in his life Albert knew what is meant by the pangs of love. He also had regained his manhood, thanks to Nellie of Shreveport, Louisiana.

"So what are we going to do?" he asked.

"You're going to court and I'm going to get ready to go home. Albert, you've got the makings of a good man in you. I hope one day you find the right woman."

That evening she took the plane home. She didn't stay a day in New York, but continued on to good ole Shreveport, Louisiana.

THE HEART OF A BOY

I woke up one morning, in my eighty-eighth year, thinking of a favorite book I had read when a boy of eight or ten. It was given me as a Christmas gift by a loving aunt. The name of the book was *The Heart of a Boy* (*Cuore* in Italian) by Edmondo de Amicis. Knowing it must be long out of print I asked my good friend Irving Stettner of *Stroker* magazine to scout around New York and see if by any chance he could find an old copy. To my amazement he did, and in a few days I received a British edition from 1904, with the same old-fashioned illustrations that were in my boy's copy.

As soon as I began reading the book tears came to my eyes. Remember, I hadn't laid eyes on the book in almost eighty years! The remarkable thing is that the book had the same impact on the man of eighty-seven as on the boy of eight or ten that I once was. (Are there any children's books like that today? I ask myself. I bloody well doubt it. Moreover children of that age today are not reading but watching television, than which nothing could be more disastrous.)

I called it a boy's book, but actually it is also an adult's book. In fact I am not sure but what its message was and still is meant for adults rather than children.

Before I go on let me recount a curious thing about this book. It was lying on my table half open when I received an unexpected visit from my Vietnamese translator. (He was a boat refugee.) During our talk he noticed the book, picked it up, and exclaimed, "Why I read this book (in French) as a boy of ten in Vietnam." And the following day I had a woman visitor, a Swiss-Italian raised in the vicinity of Locarno (in the Ticino) who also had read the book—in Italian. She told me she believed it was still being read by Italian school children today.

I am writing about this little-known book in the hope that some more people will tell me where to get more copies of the book. (I want to give it to a few friends as a gift.)

Needless to say, it is not only sentimental but also moralistic. There are the good guys and the bad guys. It all takes place in an Italian village. It is the account of a year (probably the author's) in an elementary school. There is patriotism (recollections of Garibaldi), and heroism and scoundrelism. Every type of boy imaginable, rich and poor, healthy and crippled, studious and dullard, lazy and industrious. Each chapter is about an "event" which illustrates one phase of character after another. Above all there is tenderness, great tenderness, something which D. H. Lawrence often referred to.

The master is sombre but not stern. He loves his pupils and is beloved by them. Sometimes the pupils come to the master's rescue. In any case, though they are thoroughly *boys* (boys will be boys) they do not in the least resemble the school kids of today. Today a teacher not only has to know his subjects but he has to be skilled in the martial arts as well. He is dealing, especially in the big cities, with incipient criminals. He is dealing with youngsters who already are familiar with the language of *Tropic of Cancer* and worse. He is dealing with children who have already had sexual intercourse with their feminine classmates.

When I was a boy such a state of affairs was unknown. No one would dare raise a hand against a teacher. If some teachers happened to be homosexual we were not aware of it. It was *we* who got slapped around—*at home.*

Perhaps the most striking feature of this book was its portrayal of a little cosmos. There was every kind of boy in these class rooms. Sometimes I think that it was this picture of a miniature society in which all types existed in nearly harmonious accord that led me to so readily take to Socialism and Anarchism. In my youth, in Brooklyn, the hobo was a fairly customary sight. He was usually an anarchist without portfolio, so to speak. He had rejected our phony civilized way of life and taken up the life of an exile.

Some could have made good Franciscans. They were no longer interested in changing the world, they had changed worlds. I knew a few much later in life, all of whom were virtually Christ-like figures, albeit a bit lousy, a bit filthy (more, indeed, like the monks of the Dark Ages).

What I mean to say by all this is that this little Italian school room gave me my first picture of the world-as-is. By the time I reached grammar school I found a world divided—rich vs. poor, Gentile vs. Jew, scholar vs. ordinary student, to say nothing of Republican vs. Democrat and so on. In short, that beautiful cosmos in which everyone had a part no longer existed. When I began to read this book, just recently, I had hopes that perhaps by reviewing it in the book columns I might stir up renewed interest and see it republished. I thought especially of how it might affect our young readers.

Today I no longer entertain such a hope. Our youngsters, like our adults, are doomed. Too late to turn back the tide. Too late for conversion. We are in the last stages of civilization—there is no recovery from arteriosclerosis.

Let the do-gooders die in harness. The rest of us may as well fold our hands and await the death knell. We already speak, as did the Bible of old, of "the living dead." This is the most horrible death of all—death in life. So be it. Amen!

A FEW CHAOTIC RECOLLECTIONS

Over the mirror in my bathroom is a reproduction of a Tahitian painting by Gauguin, in which one may read the French words: "D'où suis-je venu?" "Où allons-nous?" and, I believe also "Que faisons-nous ici-bas?" To translate—"Where do I come from?" "Where are we going?" "What are we doing here below?"

To these fundamental queries I might add: Who or what is God? How did the Universe come about? What happens after death?

These last, as well as the former by Gauguin, plagued me during most of my life. To this day I cannot say I have found the answers. I no longer try. I prefer to abide in mystery. To me *everything* partakes of mystery. To me neither the rational–minded nor the religious–minded have found suitable explanations.

Yet, a name like that of Nostradamus always strikes a responsive chord in me. I consider his prophecies covering a span of many centuries authentic. I cannot give a reason why. I have visited his birthplace and met, in Sarlat, a remarkable physician who wrote a wonderful book about Nostradamus and his prophecies. The name of this physician was Dr. de Fontbrune. When I met him he told me that his interest in Nostradamus was aroused by talks with a Spanish patient of his, an ordinary individual, as best I remember. We had many long talks and some correspondence too.

My interest in Dr. de Fontbrune's book came about through a chance visit to the old town of Sarlat in the South of France. The book was on display in the show window. As I was looking at it the owner of the book store came out to pull down the shutters for the night. Discovering that I was an American, a writer, and interested in Nostradamus, he immediately made me a gift of the book (a rather expensive one) and invited me to dinner.

Some years later, traveling thru France with my brother-in-law Bezalel Schatz of Jerusalem we stopped to pay our respects to the doctor. Lilik, as I called my brother-in-law, was a thorough scep-tic. He became increasingly so when the doctor reported Nostra-damus' glum views about Israel. I remember Lilik turning away in disgust, and repeating, "Never, never! Impossible!" (I wonder what he would say today if he were still alive?)

Anyway, while leading what most people would call "an ad-venturous life," what was always uppermost in my mind, taking precedence even over cunt, were these fundamental questions—Why are we here? Where are we going? What's the meaning of it all? I know the readers of *Tropic of Cancer* may find this diffi-cult to swallow. . . . They are still wallowing in cunt, fuck, shit, etc.

And one other big question—"Who am I?" From early on I am asking my elders these questions, and getting nowhere. Even at this early age I am beginning to suspect that no one has the answers, and particularly *not* those who *pretend* to have them! The know-it-alls! How I detested them!

Concomitant with these problems was the growing conviction that the scientists were full of shit. I had not yet experienced any miracles but I was prepared to accept them. I was more interested in miracles than in so-called reality. Later, of course, I came to realize that reality and truth were things people never come to grips with.

I was also "afflicted" with *nostalgia,* whose original Greek mean-ing is "longing for the womb" and not just longing. From an early age I was somehow aware that *this* was not the right place. By this, I mean the "world" that men have created. Life I always found marvelous; I might even say *divine.* But humanity, no! Humanity stank. Humanity did not deserve the life it was offered. Later, when I came to read about the Gnostics, I fully agreed with a saying accredited to them, vis., that "the planet Earth is a cosmic error." And last of all perhaps I began to question the sanity of the Creator. Why create a race of people (called humans) who had no aptitude for the things, the experiences we call human? Did not the inferior creatures of the earth show a better example of how to cope with life? Though they may eat one another to survive they did not invent such an ignoble and insane thing as war! Only the other day, in his speech accepting the Nobel Prize, Isaac Singer made mention of the fact that Yiddish (the language he wrote his books in) did not contain a word which meant "weapons." If he had said nothing more than that I would have counted it a great speech. But the world paid no heed to it. And, sadly enough, the Jews who once spoke Yiddish have discarded it for Hebrew, the language of the Bible, and are steeped in the art of making war.

What a world we inhabit today! Whoever thinks civilization means civilization (as usually conceived) had better take another think. As Oswald Spengler pointed out at the end of the first World War, in his *Decline of the West*, civilization is equivalent to arteriosclerosis. It is the dying period of a culture. Today we see it clearly, though we may not be willing to acknowledge it. Death is the only thing we live for. How best to deliver it? Or better said—"How to dish it out?" Nowhere on this globe does there seem to be an area of peace and harmony. All is strife, confusion, mendacity, and buggery. The so-called Holy Cities are contaminated. Nowhere do we see a sign of Augustine's *City of God*.

Yet I notice from my "Travel Notes" that there were two outstanding cities which I liked—Cordova in Spain and Verona in Italy. Both romantic places, to be sure. Cordova I remember for the wondrous mosque in which the Catholics had installed a church by knocking out God knows how many pillars. An act of pure desecration. And in Verona there was an air of gaiety, of *laissez-faire*, and of *love*. It is there that the vault for Romeo and Juliet stands. In other words, fifteen or twenty years ago, when I visited these towns they seemed unspoiled by the decay of civilization. They stood out from the rest of the towns and cities of their country like oases in a desert. Throwbacks, in other words, to a more glorious epoch.

There were cities I dreamed of visiting but never made it. First and foremost Lhassa in Tibet; second, Mecca, the city forbidden to Christians and Gentiles; third Timbuktu of which I had read and heard fabulous accounts. (Once I thought a British magazine editor was going to pay my expenses to make the trip from Big Sur, California to these three cities so that I could report my impressions of them, but the scheme fell through.) I should also include Samarkand and Isfahan. The two latter places seemed even more unreachable than the other three.

12/9/78

Dear Dr. Giessel—[1]

Your unexpected holiday greetings reached me yesterday and bowled me over. Especially coming from that dead area—"the heart of Texas."

Thank you for the offer, but I am not in need of special help. I have three or four doctors, all friends, who take care of me very well. (I will be eighty-seven day after X'mas.) My sight is biggest problem—blind in one eye and the good eye not so good. But morale is steady—and, believe it or not, I am again *in love*.

I suppose you are one of my readers. But *how*, if I may ask, did I help you? Maybe it's idiotic of me to ask, but you must admit doctors don't often thank laymen for help of any kind.

All the best to *you*! I don't observe any of the damn holidays nor do I vote ever.

Sincerely,
Henry Miller

---

[1] Dr. William U. Giessel of Houston, Texas.

Dear Irving—(At last a word or two from your Capricorn friend in P.P.[1])

It makes me feel so good to know there is a comparatively unknown little magazine in the heart of Second Avenue (ghetto to the world) in which I am granted full freedom of speech. It's also ironic that someone like myself cannot find an outlet in an American magazine of any repute. To be sure, our one-time good mags have all disappeared. Everything of value is disappearing today in "the greatest country in the world." We are now in a sense "deep in the heart of Texas." (Oswald Spengler would have phrased it differently. So would Céline and Cendrars.)

Which reminds me—the other day I got a letter from one of my readers telling me that a wild Israeli à la Cendrars is about to translate the body of Cendrars' prose works, beginning with *L'Homme Foudroyé*. He says, believe it or not, that this Israeli is like Cendrars in many ways. This I find hard to swallow. But, who knows? Israel is capable of giving birth to saints, martyrs, and monsters. She did not give birth to Isaac Singer. As he would put it, because they, the Israelis speak and write Hebrew, not Yiddish. (Incidentally, whether true or exaggerated, I adore what he said about the people who use Yiddish as a language. That Yiddish is a language which has no words for weapons!!! But it has *gonof* and *schmuck* and a few other delectables, eh what?)

Today or tomorrow I am mailing you a copy of that book I mentioned by a Moslem, Mohammed Mrabet. The one called *Look and Move On*. What a kick I got out of that little book! So simple, so direct, so uncompromising. A real natural. It was sent me originally by a most intelligent fan in Salt Lake City. Who'd have thunk it? But then who would think that my best, my most enthusiastic bookseller was from Kosciusko, Miss. (moved

[1] Pacific Palisades.

now to Johnson City, Tenn., where he claims he is doing a land-office business in my books). *Oi gewalt!*

I hope, Irving, that you read Isaac B. Singer's speech of acceptance. For once a Nobel Prize winner said something. It was a *noble* speech which could only have come from a man of the Diaspora. Towards the end, he expresses the idea that possibly the poet is the hope of the world, can provide a solution for our ills. Which reminds me of Gurdjieff and his Institute for the Harmonious Development of Man. I wrote a brief preface for a new edition of Fritz's [Fritz Peters] book *Boyhood with Gurdjieff* which I have read at least three times and hereby recommend to all and sundry. What I intended to say was that after finishing the book for the third time I am more than ever convinced that there can never be any "harmonious development of man," that man belongs with the animal species and not with the cherubim and seraphim. The poet may be worlds better and more developed than the politician, the militarist, or the business man. He may even be a prophet as Singer maintains, but he ain't gonna cure man of his ills. At this point I wonder if perhaps I am not confusing the poet and the genius. I am sure the genius will never lead us out of the wilderness. The idiot, on the other hand, will always provide wisdom, entertainment, and fearlessness. But perhaps the poet is a breed I am less familiar with. In all my life I have only encountered two or three—and they were not writers.

Another book I took to my bosom was a pictorial biography of Hermann Hesse. He writes a twenty page preface, telling of his life—and it is simply grand. He touches on a chord very close to my heart. The business of "Superiority." He admits that, though he may have been right (as in refusing to fight in World War One), though he may have been an inspiration to his readers, was he after all so very different from his fellow men whom he ridiculed, criticized, and condemned? Was he not born of "Protestant" parents? In my latter years I have gone over the same ground in my mind. *Who the hell do I think I am?* But, Irv, no matter how I argue, I am what I am and no one can take that away from me; moreover, *I know who I am*, which is another way of saying "Fuck you, Jack, I'm not joining your band-wagon. Not even if you are a Zen Buddhist." Hesse gave me *Siddhartha*, for which I am eternally grateful. And because of that wonderful book, I not only killed in me the Jesus, the Buddha, the Mahomet, but the guy I once thought I was and who was just another horse's ass. In short, I became myself.

At this point I have to take a rest. My eye won't let me go on. But I'll come back after a rest 'cause I have more to tell you. (Don't let me forget to tell you about your latest water color—and *Munakata*.)

For three days now I have been receiving tons of mail from idiots who haven't the remotest connection with that poor Jew, Jesus the Christ. So, business is better than ever, and every fucking Christian (or Jew or Mohammedan) feels a little less guilty. (All bathed in the blood of the Lamb, what Ho!) But fuck the Yuletide spirit. Let me tell you about Munakata and the effect he is having upon me.

About ten or twelve years ago a friend of the family—an artist— made me a gift of a pocket book on Munakata, the modern Japanese artist (now dead). The other day as a gift I received from a Japanese woman a handsome album full of reproductions of this same man's work. He was so nearsighted that his nose virtually touched the material he was working with, flat on his stomach. But he hardly needed those two myopic eyes. He had other better eyes which introduced and interspersed the most heteroclite objects and creatures and calligraphy. When you open this album at random you are hit in the face with color, line, chaos, song, poetry, everything imaginable. It is a far cry from the *ukiyoe* of Hokusai and Hiroshige. A far cry too from the *Guernica* of Picasso. Nor are his females reminiscent of Utamaro or Renoir. This is the work of an inspired lunatic. God bless him! I have ordered some copies of the pocket edition from Tuttle &

Co. in Vermont and will send you one soon as I receive them. Meanwhile I am doing some imitation Munakatas. If only we had a calligraphy on the order of Chinese-Japanese! What a sheer delight to form these characters. And to think that every hook, curve, and twist in the writing of a word has its own separate meaning! How naif we are, how childish, how uninspired. By the way, earlier I referred to Mohammed Mrabet as a Moslem. He is a Moroccan from Tangiers. Perhaps he's also a Moslem. Maybe just a *yenta*. In any case, strong brew. He fucks right and left, anything with a cunt. And no qualms, no questions, no analysis. He fucks men too, like any good Moslem. You'll get a kick out of this book. It's a lesson in "how to write" for young *and* old writers.

My Brenda is at this moment in Hattiesburg, Miss. on her way to Rio for a brief vacation. Lucky gal! You are marooned in your ghetto and I'm in my "Greek Mansion" (according to Kazin). You are the better off. When I look at your latest water color I know you are in good spirits, despite X'mas, Hanukkah, and all the fucking holidays. I wish I could say go visit the Houston Street Burlesk on the 25th but I'm afraid it no longer exists. I was thinking of "The Roseland" (dance hall) the other day and wondering how they dance there these days—cheek to cheek or just orgiastic solos. No more Fletcher Henderson either, no doubt. (Are there any dance halls in your area? Are the good old cafes still there? Fruitless questions, no doubt.)

And now to come to your latest *aquarelle*. Superb! A new freedom you have found, along with the ghost of an elephant. He seems to be trumpeting—probably the blues. Anyway, you have loosened up considerably. Color excellent. As usual you include a bit of everything—hummingbirds, mountain oysters, crabs' legs, whangdoodles, open and closed vaginas, tarts' tits, and what not. Munakata will refurbish your painting vocabulary. (By the way, at table the other night our friend Sava, looking at all your *aquarelles*, said—That guy is a real poet. He didn't mean a versifier but a Poet with a capital P.)

Everyone who dines with me notices your work, and they all express their admiration for your verve and your freedom. When you wrote me you were peddling your water colors from cafe to cafe I was extremely touched. Mostly I thought—what a lucky guy to be put to such tactics! How beautiful to be intelligent, an artist, and stone broke. You never asked me for a penny either. And, Irving, I feel a bit guilty that I didn't offer to help you. But, as I said above, I rather envied you. Yours is the *life*. It reminds me somehow of *Narcissus and Goldmund* by Hesse! The priest admitting that the adventurer (or sinner) had led the better life.

And this, though inapropos, reminds me of a remark made by a friend about Singer's work. Seems that he has been translated into Japanese (probably from his English translations)—I can't imagine any Jap reading or writing Yiddish. Yet my friend Kai Ueno of Ichinoseki knew Hebrew as well as five or six other languages, including Finnish (sic). The excruciating thing, according to my friend, is that Singer's work is highly admired by the Japanese. Droll, eh?

Today I received a book from the publisher—*Love Signs* by a woman astrologer. I immediately looked up the section I am interested in. Came to a strange conclusion. That friendship dissolves all sects, cults, races, enemies, religions, and astrological mastery. As you know, people usually resort to astrology in despair or desperation. They expect *hope* if not miracles. And the astrologer can only give what is—or to put it another way, *what gives*. He can't say—"You'd be better off going with a Leo or whatever instead of the person you have chosen." What shit, to pretend to know who you'd be better off with! Haven't we all had the experience of falling in love or in friendship with the despised, the criminal, the outcast, and finding him or her just marvelous?

Just as there ain't no hope for "the harmonious development of man," so there is always the possibility of a miracle. Only the miraculous is worth talking about, what what! At least, that's how I see it nowadays.

And so, my dear Irving and your *Stroker*, continue to live the miraculous lives you always have. You may be the Patrol of Second Avenue but you are King (like Sinatra) in your own realm. Long live *Stroker*! And you, my friend, don't ever hesitate to ask me for help! How is Tommy doing these days? He should read Mohammed Mrabet's *Harmless Poisons and Blameless Sins* (pub. by Black Sparrow Press, Santa Barbara). This letter was not dictated by any fucking Xmas or Hanukkah spirit but just by a strong feeling of friendship.

Ever yours,
Henry

"I PISS ON IT ALL FROM A CONSIDERABLE HEIGHT." L. F. Céline

Dear Irving—

Sandy, my sec'y, is typing a hand-written letter to you (eleven pages) touching on a number of things of mutual interest. I *believe* you may want to publish it in *Stroker*. If so, would you mind if I sent a copy to Shiro Hayashi, a good friend in Tokyo, who runs a popular literary mag. there? I have already written him about the idea.

Also, to help make your *Stroker* better known, I'd like to help pay for that issue by taking twenty-five or more copies which I would mail out to a select few. How much would you charge me for that many copies? (The postage on your last issue—first class— was 42¢. Can it go any cheaper? Sandy doubts it—she has the dope from P.O.) Anyway, I like the idea of writing for *your* mag. (for nothing) rather than some big shit of a mag. Have ten *very* short stories in hands of a new agent to sell to mags. Over a month since I gave her them—no response. The stories I mean are chapters from coming Vol. III (*Book of Friends*). They are about women I never slept with—i.e. *none* of the ten are. Sort of O'Henry surprise endings. Anyway, let me know when you have time.

Henry

Ps. It's X'mas and Hanukkah today, I believe, but you'd never know it here. All's quiet as the proverbial mouse. Only your water color *sings out*! CHEERS!!!

Dear Irv—

The setup for #10 looks good. I am most curious about your Sologub item. He's the man who wrote a book called A *Gob of Spit*, did you know that?

Just finished reading that Pierre Loti book you so kindly sent me.[1] Did I ever pay you for it? I forget. It requires great patience to read but is worth the effort. A *real* romance. And in Turkey of all places. I read it maybe sixty years ago. Will never forget it. He may be outdated, our Pierre Loti, but he could paint characters and scenes. If you ever get the time, try it. We don't see books like this or like *Cuore* any more. The men who made them belong to a vanished race.

So long now!

Henry

More for *Stroker* coming next week.

---

[1] *The Disenchanted* by Pierre Loti.

Dear Irv—

Your very very wonderful water color arrived yesterday. I was going to send you a telegram congratulating you but then came all sorts of interferences. I think it the best of your work I have seen so far. (Maybe Anna's presence has something to do with it!)

You're right, it is *different* from your previous work. The others betray the "sketcher" a bit; this is pure free painting. Congratulations—you are now on the road.

I was touched that you sent it *framed*—thank you again. You're a prince (only the poor know how to be generous to a fault).

Irv, yes, if you could conveniently *type* letters, it would be better. You have a rather raggedy scrawl, if you don't mind my saying so.

I'm going to ask Brenda if she has a poem I once sent her. It may be *good*. I can't tell about poetry myself.

Interesting about those ad places for *Stroker*. You may yet make it a profitable venture. This in haste. More later.

Henry

Thursday, March 1979

Dear Irving,

This is a sort of Easter greeting to you, though I am no more a Christian than you are a Jew. Somehow we were fortunate enough to escape the "wheel of religion." By which I mean—the Ferris wheel which takes you nowhere. Often beautiful objects, like the one in Vienna, but heal no wounds, mend no bones or broken hearts.

Today I received *three* letters in a row from you. Happy Easter! The one you enclosed from Paul Bowles about Mrabet I liked very much. He sounds like a truly civilized man, as was Marcel Duchamp. (Ever meet him in Paris?) I once tried to play a game of chess with him—at his urgent request. What a fiasco!

Anyway, I am writing to encourage you to keep *Stroker* alive. It is beginning to reach the right people, I feel. I want to send you names of more prospects, and I will, soon as I can make time. You are on the right track. (Second Ave. Patrol.) From that ghetto you can reach the world far better than a Madison Avenue address, believe me. Madison Ave. and Park Ave. have an ominous ring to me. One spells chicanery; the other, luxurious waste. *Ennahow.* . . .

My dear friend Twinka Thiebaud, daughter of the famous American painter, has been writing a book for the last year or so, based on dinner conversations with me *chez moi*. She used to cook meals for me and keep house for several years. She is very attractive, was an artist's model for a while, and had ambitions for stage and cinema. But living in this household, listening so much to my babble, she finally abandoned all her plans and decided to become a writer.

She has to date fifty chapters of *my* talk at table, imitating my style, my hems and haws—all without using a tape recorder. I am going to ask her next week if she would care to send one chapter to you for *Stroker*. Will suggest first chapter, which deals with

Death. (Very appropriate for the season, *quoi!*) Should have included Resurrection but doubt I did.

Listen, it's only my talk—she doesn't give her questions. But one can read between the lines. I think it's excellent and I hope to find a publisher for her here on the Coast.

I am almost through proofreading *Joey*.[1] It's about Alfred. Perles, plus a few short anecdotes on some bizarre episodes with other sex.

Have to quit here, Irv. Eyes give out easily.

Easter! Where did that fucking name originate? In French c'est *Pâques*, comme vous savez.

Alors, fuck a duck! Lay a good Easter Egg—a kosher one!

Henry

[1] *Book of Friends*, Vol. III.

Dear Irv—

Forgot to tell you Warren Beatty would like to use me as a "Voice" (talking about N.Y.C. 1915–1920) in forthcoming film *Ten Days that Shook the World*[1] (by John Reed). Film *not* based on his book but his love affair with Louise Strong, his collaborator. Wants to see me here about June 20th.

Last night, 3 A.M. I began to get nervous. How well do I recall N.Y. of that period. Enclose hasty notes I made, which please return when you reply.

What I'd like is if you could let me know title & pub. of a book covering N.Y. at that time (World War I). Then Sava could borrow a copy from Beverly Hills Library!

Am not sure I'll do it. Wrote his "historical consultant" I was no prof, no scholar, no historian. He may not like my reply to his invitation. Best is, Beatty promised to find job for Brenda in coming film, not this one. I made that one of my conditions.

Hope I'm not burdening you. But you're such a good sleuth!

Cheers!

Henry

---

[1] Title later changed to *Reds*.

Midnight 3/31/79

Dear Irv—

Just a quickie to say you can keep that Augustine script. I have two more copies. (Happy to know you are interested at all. Augustine sounds great. Ever read him—his *Confessions* or *The City of God?*) Why don't you write Donald Nugent, the author— Head of English Dept. at University of Kentucky—Louisville, Ky. Tell him you're a good friend of mine. Send him *Stroker* #8. (They are performing play at the school.) But he might be pleased if you offered to publish it in *Stroker*. I don't think he needs money. Say you can't afford to pay for contributions yet but will one day. Tell him you are a perpetual and peripatetic poet who makes beautiful WC's (according to H.M.) on the side. His letters give impression of a good egg. But with "Academics" you just never can tell. No harm trying, though.

Hope to give you names & addresses to circularize soon. Sava here tonight to make dinner. He loves you, thinks you're the cat's whiskers . . . Don't lose that phrase—"The 2nd Ave. Patrol"—I love it. "The peripatetic poet" ain't bad either, eh? Off to bed now. Vive *Stroker!* A bas les grandes revues! Ca y'est!

Henry

Ps. Great if you could dig up two more *Cuore*. I've got a dozen sleuths looking for copies. You will love it and want to reprint some of it, I'm sure.

Dear Irving —

First off—here is a check for the three copies of *Cuore*.[1] Why should *you* pay? I'm trying to help *you* and *Stroker*.

By all means print "Mes Hommes à Moi" and, if you have extra copies of that small repro. send me two please. But don't bother to print new ones if you don't happen to have copies.

Am a little confused by your remark—"Can't print Schnellock letter." I only sent you "The Painting Lesson." Will you be able to publish that next time or this time or any time? About a friend who is interested—I'll let you know when I hear from him. I *hate* any one *editing* my work.

I thought I sent you a third piece to publish in *Stroker* some-time—forgot what now. *May* have an excerpt from *Joey* for you *soon*. Finishing proofreading tonight. Loads of errors. Noel has a drunken printer, I'm told. Bad biz, what!

(Sent you a colored repro. from Japan of a mysterious W.C. I don't know when or where I made it.)

Give my best to Anna. Glad you are still together. Happy days! Cheers!

This at top speed—so much to do. All my thanks, Irv, for all your many kindnesses and best from Sava who really appreciates you. *Vive Stroker!*

Henry

---

[1] *Heart of a Boy* (English transl.) by Edmondo De Amicis.

5/17/79

Dear Irv—

Got your letter and water color today. Eye still bad. Waiting for doctor from St. Barbara. Is he on your list for *Stroker*? He's a reader and collector. Dr. James F. O'Roark—Santa Barbara, Ca.

What I'm really writing you about is this. Pat Eddingtcn of Salt Lake City (one of your subscribers, I believe) keeps asking me about those drawings I made for T.T. "Open Letter to *Stroker*." There are three he would like—I think to buy. I don't believe I have any more of the large size ones. Do you? If so, would you mind asking which *three* he wants and sending them to him? Don't charge him. Charge ME!

I was surprised you thought so well of "Vienna and Back." I had first called it "Love and Sex" but then remembered doing a piece by that very title for some Greenwich Village book store.

Your water color this time did not impress me so much—maybe because of my bad sight. You sure turn them out fast. Reichel used to take lots of time with his. Linger over them a little more. After W.C. dries go to it with colored inks or just black ink. Sort of *against the grain*—in other words, not *harmoniously*. Gives great results, so I think.

Irv, I'm still waiting for eye doctor to come see me. Still crippled! Don't know how I manage to write this well.

Cheers!

Henry

Do you know the difference between titillate and *titivate*? I wrote Capra for permission to send you the short women's stories that go in *Joey* book. Right up your alley. I hope he has no objections. Keep the aspidistra flying. Best to Anna.

Tuesday
[undated, 1979]

Dear Irv—

Enclosing a piece called "Asamara" (or "morning erection" in Japanese). Should be at top of page. And maybe footnote at bottom explaining that it is real Japanese word for "morning erection." I wrote it to go with a W.C. I did (a rare one of a guy with an erection—but a modest one).

Irv—that letter about printing special issue I will show to Sava Saturday when he cooks for me. (If I can find it! Am simply overrun with mail—in several languages.)

You mentioned Chaplin. I have a wonderful story to tell about meeting him at Simenon's home in Switzerland. What an evening! Did I ever tell you about it?

Glad you liked "Memory & Forgettery" so much. My sec'y on the contrary thought it one of the least interesting things I sent you.

Irv, I just can't keep up with you. You seem to be everywhere, know everybody, and can do any damned thing.

That book on N.Y.—would you like it? I won't be consulting it any more. In fact, I discovered later I didn't need it. Beatty didn't want *factual* information—only impressions and feelings. We talked for three and a half hours. He was delighted. Told Brenda next day—"I just love that H.M." I liked him too. Much better than I had anticipated. You know what the film's about—John Reed and Louise Strong—love affair. Not the book. Not Eisenstein's film! Well, you'll probably see it in a couple of months.

Noel Young (Capra) was here yesterday. That book on W.C.'s is coming along. Needs capital and co-publishers.

Thanks so much Irv for all you have done and are doing. *Stroker* will make a name for itself, you'll see.

Henry

P.S. Oh yes. I always forget—give my best to your printer friend, "Isadore" Cohen!

P.P.S. And thanks for that little print of the W.C. Looks very sharp!

ASAMARA

Lovers engaged in fornication sometimes experience a miss-fire reaction. This can come about through failing to take the azimuth correctly. Failing to take the azimuth correctly affects the morning erection or *Asamara*, as the Japanese prefer to call it. As a consequence the spermatozoa are apt to go astray in the stratosphere. Such occurrences need cause no alarm if the participants are penitent and endeavor to remain in a state of orgiastic fury.

Nature takes no notice of human miscalculations. The world of monsters and misfits falls under the sway of cosmic law just as does the world of saints, eunuchs, and bedbugs.

What the artist struggles to depict is a state of mind. He knows that lovers are never losers. At the worst there is regression to the autonomic level where zero is equated with infinity and no questions asked.

Thereafter, for reasons inexplicable, erections follow in logical and biological sequence, often aided and abetted by an ordinary alarm clock. Taking the azimuth again becomes a pleasant habit and is not necessarily followed by hallucinations or indulgence in masturbation.

Thus, from *Asamara* to *Sayonara* is but a step, with the Mikado always holding the trump card.

These observations are offered gratuitously and need not be taken literally unless so desired.

Dear Irv—

Feeling somewhat better. Can reply to your good letter. First, you can print all three of women's stories if you like—in one issue. Sorry you prefer Renate—my favorites are Melpo & Sevasty. No, it's not the same Swami. Mine had an ashram in L.A. Wonderful man.

Sure you can use my "Linear Fantasy" in *Stroker*. That W.C. litho—was that one from Japan, done recently? I made it in 1955—can't believe it!

What does that mean—exchange subscriptions (Dutch mag)? Is the mag any good? All the creeps are going to Amsterdam today as they did to Paris in the '30's. Reason—drugs and cunt.

Barbara Kraft here last night. Made me the most wonderful filet mignon *I had ever anywhere*! (I have sixteen voluntary cooks on my list now. Barbara is the best. And a damn good woman. She's going to send you more stuff for *Stroker*.)

I am contemplating writing something for you on "Memory and Forgettery."[1] Especially the latter.

Must close now. Good to be alive, even if half blind and deaf.

Henry

P.S. Don't let *Stroker* die. When you need help (financial) call on me. Fuck the intellectual critics. I myself have criticisms—especially of the poets. You're the one and only poet America has!!!

---

[1] Printed in *Stroker* #11

My dear good friend—[1]

I was delighted to receive your wonderful letter today. I am replying immediately. The fact that you can not read has perhaps made you a better writer than most who do read. Today in this so-called "civilized" world there seems to be nothing but trash and trivia written. Like you, I was rejected and despised in my country until I was almost sixty years old. And poor as a churchmouse all those years.

Your writing is quite unique and an inspiration not only to young writers but to veterans too. You have found the secret of communicating with people on all levels. Good writers esteem you and sing your praises, at least in the western world. I wonder if you are known in France? If you have not been published there let me know and I will tell your American publisher (or perhaps your Moroccan publisher) who to contact in Paris. I think the French will love you because you are just what they need.

I am blind in one eye now and can no longer use the machine, nor read as much as I would like. I hope you or your friend can read my handwriting. The quote below is in Portugese. It is a Brazilian proverb. In English it means: "When shit acquires value the poor will be born without ass-holes."

Please give my warm greetings to Paul Bowles if you still see him.

That fable about the saint and the ignorant woman was a beauty.

One little question—are my books read in your country in French?

I close now, urging you to continue. The better you are as a writer the longer it takes to be recognized and accepted. I have lived like an outlaw most of my life. You have the right philoso-

---

[1] Mohammed Mrabet.

phy and I think you are lucky perhaps in not having the usual education.

Sincerely,
Henry Miller

QUANDO MERDA TIVER VALOR POBRE NASCE SEM CU

Friend—.
    I can either answer your letter or try to print another water color, which does my soul good.
    If you don't hear from me you will know what I have chosen to do.

                    H. M.

Henry Miller received so much mail there was simply not time to answer all of it. His secretary sometimes sent copies of this note by way of reply.

Dear Irv—

Just had letter from Bert Mathieu telling me that our word "fascination" comes from the Hittite word for vagina. (As nostalgia from "longing for womb" in Greek.)

I don't mind signing fifty or a hundred copies of *Stroker* but I wouldn't be able to dispose of them. Can't *you*? Give me perhaps a half-dozen.

By the way, Tommy's painting arrived with the glass shattered. Did you not tell me to send him, via Charlee, $130? That's what I'm doing anyhow.

Do you recall the Yiddish or Hebrew word for the thirty-two or thirty-six men born in every generation who keep the world from falling apart?[1] Not men with big names — usually unknown men, according to my departed friend Lilik Schatz. Would like to know!

Irv—why don't you write Edith Sorel yourself? I am so overloaded with letters to answer. Say I am *d'accord*, but that I don't feel capable of translating any more than you. Tell her how you used to play pinball with Tristan Tzara in Paris in the 1930s.[2]

One last question: where and when did we meet, do you remember?

Cheers now! *Stroker 11* will break the ice. Never say die!

Henry

P.S. Here's another prospect. Sent him copy of No. 11 today— John Walker, Maplewood, N.J.

[1] Refers to Lamed Vovnicks
[2] Should be the 1950s.

Dear Irv—

Got your good letter of 8/11/79. Now I have to ask if you know hour of birth—for horoscope. (It's a speculative biz—not sure of anything yet.) But I'm happy to see you are a Scorpio. So is Val 11/9 and Brenda 11/10. Good sign—for me anyway—I have three planets in conjunction there! (But I'm a Capricorn.)

Bushwick Avenue! My God! Where on Bushwick? I know it pretty well from Myrtle Ave to Evergreen Cemetery and Trommer's Beer Garden opposite. Do let me know near what street. I lived on Decatur St. bet. Evergreen and Bushwick Avenues.

You're right about spelling of Swami's name! "None but the Lonely Heart"—Jesus! I saw that years later with Tom Schiller. Here's a verse from it they sang—

"Nur wer die Sehn sucht kennst
Weisst was ist die Leide."

You and Frankel & Trotsky in Mexico! Fabulous!

Just had card from Christine Nazareth. Will be seeing *you* soon she writes. Great gal. A dynamo. Another person who aims to visit you soon is my friend Bert Mathieu who wrote *Orpheus in Bklyn*. After listening to me tell about you (the Yiddisher Rimbaud) he says—"I'm going to look him up when I get home." He's now back in Conn. You'll find him a very unusual guy, albeit a scholar!

Not worrying about Nobel Prize. I know the contenders. I'll probably be fucked again.

Must stop. Like you, I have the writer's itch.

Henry

Ps. No *Strokers* yet!!!

THE THEATRE

My earliest remembrance of any theatre is that of the vaudeville house called "The Novelty" not far from our home on Driggs Avenue, Williamsburg. Every Saturday my mother would give me a dime to buy a seat in "Nigger Heaven," as the gallery was called. I was then seven or eight years old. If there were any comedians in those days I don't recall them, or else their jokes were over my head. Mainly there were acrobats, trick cyclists, magicians, and such like.

At this same theatre, a few years later, my mother took me to see *Uncle Tom's Cabin*. This time we sat in the orchestra. Though it was then considered quite a famous play I recall viewing it with a bored attitude. "Rather childish," is what I thought to myself. When Little Eva is escaping and crossing the ice I suddenly discover that my mother is weeping. I shake her gently and whisper (rather loudly) "Mamma, it's only a play!" To have made such a remark at my tender age astounds me now. I must have been a spoiled brat.

It's during my adolescence (twelve–fifteen years of age) that I become aware of all the theatres there are or were in Brooklyn. By this time we are living in the Bushwick section, not so very far from Evergreen Cemetery, and Trommer's Beer Garden. My mother's friends often came to the house of an afternoon to attend a *Kaffee Klatsch* (coffee party.) I would listen in on the table conversation which often concerned the theatre. Thus I discovered that in the East New York section there were several 10-20-30¢ theatres, featuring shows like *Bertha the Sewing Machine Girl* or *The Two Orphans*. Now and then my mother took me to one of these performances. I was even more bored than watching *Uncle Tom's Cabin*.

In another section of town, near the Old Neighborhood, was a quite famous little theatre run by an eccentric ham actor named Corse Payton whom my old man used to get drunk with later when Payton began patronizing the Hotel Wolcott Bar. Here there were grandiose melodramas given, with Corse Payton always in the leading role. His repertoire might include *The Count of Monte Cristo* or *Les Misérables* or *Hamlet* or *Othello*. Today this entire neighborhood has been taken over by Chassidic Jews from the lower East Side. An extraordinary change, to say the least.

There was one other play my mother took me to when I was about twelve or fourteen—and I have never forgotten it. That was *Wine, Women, and Song* with Lew Ahearn, a real zany. The title of this musical comedy reminds me of an old German verse: "*Wer liebt nicht Wein, Weib und Gesang, Bleibt ein Knarr sein Leben lang.*" Translated—"Who loves not Wine, Women . . . song remains a fool his whole life long."

For some reason this play tickled me enormously. Lew Ahearn was probably the first droll creature I ever saw on stage. His antics (always a bit risqué) had me in stitches. And then there were all those wonderful females, half-naked, seductive, bewitching. (A prelude to the burlesque which I was later to patronize avidly.)

Why my Puritanical mother ever took me to see a performance of this sort is still a mystery to me. I must mention that the theatre in which it was shown was called "The Follies," comer of Broadway and Graham Avenue, not so far from the home of my first love.

In the heart of the shopping district, on Fulton Street was a classy theatre called "The Orpheum." There one saw more serious, more tragic, more sophisticated plays, or a tender, romantic play, like *Rebecca of Sunnybrook Farm* might be the show, starring a well-known actress named Edith or Mabel Taliaferro. Her photo, life-size, used to be plastered on the fence near Bushwick Avenue and Decatur St. On my way home from school I would stand a few minutes and gaze at her in rapture.

I recall that about this time there was a play which was considered quite *avant-garde* then. It was called *The Witching Hour* by Kyrle Bellew. There was also a director and actor, very famous, who dressed like a priest and who had as a mistress a rather stunning actress, whose virtue was not of the highest repute. A famous line of his was often repeated here and there—"If *you* don't want her *I* want her!" delivered in a melodramatic tone. I am talking of David Warfield in *The Music Master.*

One of the strangest evenings I ever spent at the theatre was with my old man. Apparently one of his customers (an actor) had given him two orchestra seats for a play at the famous Herald Square Theatre called *A Gentleman from Mississippi.* And who should be the "gentleman" but Fatty Arbuckle who was later to earn a bad name in the film business. What the play was all about I no longer remember. It seemed to me that the drama had little to do with the title. Mississippi, of course, held a great charm for me. It was a Romantic State redolent of "The War Between the States," as the Southerners rightly called it. It had associations with Mark Twain; it boasted fabulous mansions, as well as trees and plants unheard of up North. But none of all this fantasy seemed to have crept into the script. However, for me, it was an event. It was the first time in my young life that I had set foot in a *Broadway* theatre.

In this same period, between sixteen and eighteen years of age, I also frequented a theatre called "The Broadway" at Flushing Avenue and Broadway, Brooklyn. This theatre showed plays that had been hits on Broadway (N.Y.) a year or two earlier. I used to go with a friend named Bob Haas. We stood up in the rear of the theatre, paying only fifty cents admission. Here for the first time in our lives we saw some really first rate plays and excellent actors and actresses. (Some of the latter were from Europe, usually France.) We had to walk back and forth from our homes to the theatre—several miles each way. During these walks home we would discuss the performance we had witnessed, criticize the actors and the playwrights. It was wonderful exercise for our young minds.

I believe it was here, or was it later at the Theatre Guild that we attended plays by Shaw, O'Neill, and various British playwrights.

But before I come to the Theatre Guild I have some ground to traverse. Before the Theatre Guild came into being we had two very interesting attempts at non-commercial theatre. One was the Washington Square Players and the other was the Neighborhood Playhouse on the lower East Side. In between was the Henry Street Settlement, run by young teen-age amateurs. Here one night I saw a performance of one of Shakespeare's plays such as I have never seen before or after. And the actors were all of that very poor neighborhood, the sons and daughters of lowly immigrants. I left the theatre as if walking on eggs. My ears were still ringing with the melodious lines I had heard from untrained lips. It was incredible. It proved to me what could be done with very little. It made all the glamorous Broadway productions look shabby, contrived, and utterly unimaginative.

The Neighborhood Playhouse had the same authenticity but was more sophisticated and could afford well-trained actors. I recall vividly my first visit—they were giving a play by a well-known British author who had encouraged Joseph Conrad to be a writer and to write in English rather than Polish or French. It happened that night that the leading actress was the beautiful, mature wife of the well-known Richard Bennett. The scene which electrified me was of her sitting in her boudoir before her make-up table, dressed rather scantily and glorious to behold. What got me was that she sat there, looking at herself in the mirror and never uttering a word. Everything that passed through her mind was registered in her facial expressions. Shadows flitted across her face, her eyes flashed, her teeth shone white and bright, her hands made gesticulating motions. It was hallucinating. I had never seen such acting before.

And so, when I arrived home, I sat down and wrote her a eulogistic letter. I must have put a return address on the envelope because in short order I received a most gracious invitation from her to come visit her in her dressing room.

Of course, I didn't go. I could not conceive of a gawk such as myself holding conversation with a lady of her stature.

In the case of the Washington Square Players I happened to know two of the company, and neither the man nor the woman seemed like actors to me. (In all fairness I must admit that at that age I thought of actors as very exceptional people, endowed, like musicians, with a great gift.) In this theatre more eccentric and sophisticated plays were given. I remember the odd title of one of their plays: *Twelve who Pass While the Lentils Boil.*

With the Theatre Guild I began to see imported plays. It was the period when German Expressionism was at its height here. There were excellent productions without the usual great stars. One went for the play, not for the famous actor or actress.

A little later, after I have been initiated into the world of sex, I believe I am more attracted by the name and fame of certain actors, especially celebrated *actresses,* than by the play itself.

Oddly, one of the very first actresses with whom I became infatuated was Elsie Janis. Elsie Janis played all over Broadway. She was a perennial. She was not a raving beauty nor a great actress. In a way she was a sort of female zany. She could give improvisations in lightning-like order of Hamlet, Sarah Bernhardt, Leslie Carter, David Warfield, anyone from any walk of life. She was the first feminine comic I had seen. If she was not a raving beauty she was certainly good to look at, titillating to listen to, and unforgettable. For years she was the darling of Broadway. I feel I owe her a great deal. She broke the ice, so to speak, she linked our amateurish, dead-serious theatre to the *Commedia del Arte* kind of theatre. One left the theatre spell-bound after seeing her. She gave it a whole new dimension. And she was always alone, needed no accompaniment of any kind.

From Elsie Janis to the burlesk was a natural transition. In my early twenties I was already fed up with the American theatre.

The silent films were coming more to the fore. I had begun to go to the burlesk at the age of 16, thanks to an older boy friend. I almost pissed in my pants after that first glimpse. But soon I was traveling to Manhattan, to Hoboken, to "The Star" near Borough Hall, wherever I knew of a good group showing. And finally I found that *ne plus ultra* of burlesk—The Houston St. Burlesk, at one end of Second Avenue, N.Y. Here I was in Seventh Heaven. The comedians were not only funny, but lewd, lubricious, salacious. The women, the favorites, were equally sensual, stopping at nothing. And the orchestra leader, the guy with the red hair, was out of this world. (So much better than going to hear Paderewski!)

During my first marriage, because of the incessant bickering and quarreling with my wife, I developed migraine headaches. They were unbearable. I never thought of taking powders or going to a chiropractor. I simply put on my hat and coat and ambled off to the burlesk. By the end of the show my headache was gone. It was just like Rabelais says—"For all your ills I give you laughter."

Yes sir, *laughter*. A new and vitalizing dimension for me. I could easily have ended up a neurotic like most youngsters today. Thanks to the filth, the vulgarity, and the humor of burlesk I was saved.

Before closing I must make mention of one play which I believe affected me more than any other. And that is *Juno and the Paycock* by O'Casey.

EPILOGUE

Ever since I began writing this piece about the theatre in the back of my head has been the smoldering thought that, like music, the theatre can reach or touch us in what may be considered universal or mystical or cosmological realms.

We have long known that microscopically and macrocosmically the universe of things (bodies, matter, stars, planets, everything in short) has no limits, no boundaries. To the religious-minded this has always been a truth. The scientists, with their puny instruments are always on the search, as it were, boasting of the marvels they have uncovered or discovered. What they pretend to know about man and the universe is like a crumb in a pigeon's mouth. The full grandeur of the universe can only be apprehended emotionally. Figures mean nothing. Awareness comes in flashes, often through little things, little events.

So, in the theatre (or on film) there come these moments occasionally when one is lifted out of himself, when one knows without knowing. A gesture can provoke it, a wry smile, *anything*. Due to these "happenings" we realize that the function of the theatre is not to hand us back the everyday familiar reality but to give us intimations of a super reality which knows no bourne. Sometimes this intuition comes about by the mere presence of a certain actor or actress. They do not have to act. They do not need to do anything. Their bare presence seems to yield emanations of another order, as if they were visitors from another world. And indeed some of them definitely belong more to that other world than to this one.

Such a one, to take a single example, is Greta Garbo. She is definitely in a category all her own. People said of her that "she had *IT*." Never dreaming, of course, the full implications of such a remark. *It*, properly understood, is what governs us, not the brain or the mind. *It* is the be-all and end-all of the autonomic system, whereby our organs take care of themselves—we eat when we are hungry, we piss when our bladders are full, our heart beats of its own accord, and so on and so forth. Why therefore should the brain be any different, obeying some strange God? Every great artist will admit that *he* was not the author or composer but that *It* was. What *It* is no one knows. Any more than we know anything about the universe we are swimming in. And so, to repeat, there arrive now and then in the theatre as in the concert hall or opera house, these unique beings who have *It*. They may have gone through great training as did other artists less gifted, but they never relied on this training. The voice, the gesture, the action came from within, unbidden. Those "events," as I might call them, refresh our souls, help us endure the pallid reality of every day.

I have not dwelt on the great stars or the great playwrights, feeling that everyone has his very own. And if I dwelt rather heavily on the therapeutic value of the theatre that was not to deny the aesthetic or spiritual aspect.

I have not been to a theatre or even to a movie in a long while. I must confess I do not miss either of them. I feel I have drunk deep from the Pierian Spring. Most of the time I am not in this world, though very much of it. I fear no danger of a shortage of spiritual nourishment. Enjoy yourselves!

MEMORY AND FORGETTERY

Of the two I think it better to cultivate one's Forgettery. I know the emphasis is usually placed on memory training. But in my opinion our poor brains are overloaded with unimportant facts, with junk distributed by T.V., radio, newspapers, magazines, and a dozen other sources of useless information. One needs to unload all this garbage, not take on more.

For each person it will be another different set of baggage he wants or needs to carry through life. Certainly not what teachers, preachers, and newspaper men think important. There should be room in one's memory for the name of the first girl one fell in love with, for the first dog or cat one had, for the first time one heard of this or that astonishing thing. One can discard names and dates taught in school—especially names of battles, generals, treaties, wars. One doesn't have to be urged to remember names like Alexander the Great, Genghis Khan, Attila the Hun, Napoleon, Hitler, Robert E. Lee. Ditto for Caruso, Rimbaud, Dostoievsky, Walt Whitman, Robinson Crusoe, *Gulliver's Travels*, King Arthur. One can forget Hemingway, Scott Fitzgerald, Thurber, and their likes. But one should try to remember Sherwood Anderson and Theodore Dreiser.

One should not forget the man who renders you a wonderful service. You can forget Matthew, Mark, Luke, and John, but not the guy who got you out of a scrape or saved your life with a little chicken feed.

In my own case, as I have stated several times already, I never forget my boyish idols during the years from five to ten. Johnny Paul, who delivered coal and wood, stands out like a saint. Lester Reardon, whom I never dared approach or speak to, like Ulysses, Eddie Carney like a hero, and so on. On the other hand, the minister with the horse whip in hand, is engraved in my mind as the devil incarnate. Nor do I ever want to forget this son of a bitch. A woman like Emma Goldman remains forever in my mind as the great Teacher, Exemplar.

After people and personalities come books and their authors. They were the real influences in my life, not teachers and preachers. Whoever has read Dostoievsky knows whereof I speak.

But before getting into this subject I would like to refer back to those who are important to bear in mind. They are the little people, those without name or fame. They are the ones who keep the planet from falling apart; they are the ones who are asked to make the great, the tragic sacrifices. We are inclined to forget them too easily. The names that stick in our crop are those of the big crooks, the war mongers, the big scale assassins. One need not remember the president or ex-presidents, and certainly not the vice-presidents. One can also put in the discard all the senators, indeed all the politicians one has ever known. They only cause trouble and steal untold millions from the poor.

Likewise the sports heroes, though for my own part I can't ever forget Jack Johnson and Mohammed Ali.

There is a voluntary and an involuntary forgetting always at work. Cultivate the *voluntary* one. Never worry about forgetting what is important to remember. There are always libraries everywhere crammed with millions of books, the majority of them worthless. Avoid trying to remember facts, events, inventions, and so on. Stop reading the daily newspaper. Don't buy popular magazines or popular anything. Go only for the esoteric, the mystical, the dubious.

Believe to your heart's content. If you have faith—in no matter what—your soul will remain healthy. Don't be afraid to be a hero-worshiper. (Remember Carlyle's *Heroes and Hero Worship*.) Don't read cheap literature. Kill off the publishers who profiteer on our ignorance and credulity.

Don't look for miracles. *You* are the miracle. Free yourself of gurus, saviors, healers, and such like. Be your own savior. Above all, pay no attention to advertisements, whether in newspapers, magazines, or on walls. Resist all slogans. Avoid all healers, all wheeler-dealers. Don't *try* to remember. *Remember!* Remember to remember. Remember at all times who and what you are. Join no organizations. Take no shit, not even from Billy Graham.

Read only what you care to read, even if it is considered out-of-date or useless. The more useless the literature, the more apt it is to be great literature. Poets, in the true sense of the word, did not write to make the front page. It's the scribblers, and I don't have to mention names, who usually rake in the dough. If you find a wonderful book, make it known to your friends and comrades. Word of mouth recommendation is always the best, the strongest. Talk about the books you like, the ones which inspired you. Forget the races, politics, economics, and such like. You alone can't improve the world. The Buddha couldn't, nor Jesus, nor Mohammed. Improve yourself—that really pays off. Don't try to read a lot of books—a few good ones will suffice. Write your own books in your head. When you have found an author who captivates you, live with his work. Let him soak into your entire system, not just your brain. One author whom you are daffy about can do you more good than Jesus, Peter, Paul, and the Virgin Mary.

For my part I found two such men during my reading days— Knut Hamsun and Blaise Cendrars. I do believe to this day that Cendrars was the greatest man I ever knew of. He was everything, in addition to being a writer. He broke loose from his bourgeois home in Switzerland at about the age of sixteen. He traveled widely, read widely, spoke several languages and made friends with not only unimportant people but frequently with gangsters and murderers. He remains my hero, my idol, to this day. When I think of the great ones like Shakespeare, Milton, et alia, I think by comparison with Blaise Cendrars that they were just so much shit.

Friday
7th or 8th [1979]

Dear Irv—

It's about 4:30 PM and I'm pooped. So much clerical work to do. Forgive me for saying not to phone unless an emergency. That tells of my state of desperation. No time for self. Eyes ruined. Senseless. If this means success they can have it! It's frightful.

But all this is not what I started to tell you. Two things! 1.) You are dead right about *Stroker* run-offs of me and Brenda. Great guns! Beautifully sharp and clear.

2.) Happened to relook at two of your water colors. Never, in my confusion here, did I ever give you the proper accolade for them. They rival any French master—and surpass because of insane joy and devil may care. Now and then you pull off these *Apocatastases* (see Dict.). Fabulous. Feel I never give you enuf thanks and credit. You are my Lamed Vov and an artist for all time. Belated acknowledgement.

Brenda is going to try to find a director for film of *Smile at Foot of Ladder*. She has great hopes. I have no more illusions left. Henry will take the crumbs till he exits from stage.

Up the Booster!! Cheers

Ich gabibble!
Henry

CHILDHOOD IN BROOKLYN

Born with a silver spoon in my mouth. Got everything I craved, except a real pony. Writing Santa to send me a drum *and* a magic lantern. Returning work socks and mitten to teacher in kindergarten—to give to the poor in the class. When my mother sees me returning from kindergarten X'mas Eve and no gifts she asks what happened. I say "Nothing, I just returned them to the teacher. I know Santa is going to bring me better things." With this she slaps me hard, grabs the lobe of one ear and drags me one long block to the school, to apologize to the teacher for my rudeness.

I couldn't understand what I had done wrong. . . This was my first big misunderstanding. It registered deeply (I never forgot nor forgave) and left in my childish mind the feeling that my mother was stupid and cruel.

In later years I only slightly modified this view of my mother. She always pretended to be proud of me but she neither understood nor loved me.

More about Mother. . . .

Next to kindergarten episode, around same period, is when she shows me a wart on her finger which is annoying her and I say— "Why don't you cut it off?" And she does, gets blood poisoning, and a few days later, when I am sitting in my little chair by the fire, she comes over to me, scowling and threatening (her finger now heavily bandaged) and slaps me some more saying—"You were the one who told me to cut the wart off!"

As she lies abed, only a few days away from death, I bring my friend Vincent to see her. He is handsome, well-mannered, and an air pilot. My mother's eyes glow when she sees him. It is obvious that she has immediately taken him to heart. Suddenly she raises herself from the pillow—I am standing by the side of the bed—and exclaims: "If only I had had a son like you, Vincent," looking me in the eye while speaking. (And I was fresh from Europe where I was idolized as a great American writer. All this meant nothing to her. She never forgave me for becoming a writer instead of a tailor!)

The culminating and rather gruesome final episode takes place in a funeral parlor where she is laid out in state for her friends and relatives to say farewell to her. She is there about a week before being buried. I visit the place now and then—not everyday. Each time I come and bend over the coffin, one of her eyes opens, as if to stare at me. It seems to me she is reproving me even in death. It gives me shivers. I always notify the director of the funeral parlor who always closes the eye without saying a word.

(more or less upon actual return from
France penniless as when I left.)

EARLY DAYS

Rereading a book I read long long ago (*Heart of a Boy*) I was impressed by certain resemblances between the life of Italian boys and the ones I knew in dear old Brooklyn. For one thing we both understood what Carlyle referred to in one of his books—*Heroes and Hero Worship*. We admired the boys who inspired our admiration unashamedly. We also were hard on weaklings and dummies. Now and then we acknowledged that so-and-so was a real saint. He was apt to be six or eight years older than us, poor, hauling coal and wood for a living (this early in life), but with a golden heart. Johnny Paul, an Italian teenager, was in my humble opinion a saint; though I wasn't yet quite aware of what saints were supposed to be like. (I was brought up in a Presbyterian Church, not a Catholic one. We didn't talk of saints and Virgin Mary's there.)

We tried to win the favor of our heroes. Were they to give us a smile or a pat on the back, we were in Seventh Heaven.

In my particular neighborhood, we kids never used the word "prostitute," nor did we ever hear it. Whores was our word and one of our little girl friends was known as the whore of the neighborhood. Jenny was her name and she was a charming, gentle creature who may have shaped my image of "whore" very early in life. When I first got to Paris I made friends with the whores very readily, one of the first short stories I wrote there was about "Mlle. Claude." Somehow they were always aware that I regarded them differently than most men.

To get back to Jenny. We used to pretend to fuck her in someone's cellar—"a penny a crack." Actually all we did was to touch genitals. But we got almost as great a thrill from doing that as we did out of "a good fuck" later on.

The word I always use about my early days (from five to ten) is *golden*. In my memory this period stands out (even today) above all the others. Perhaps because everything was "new" to me. And I was a fast learner. Not only did I learn in the street but at home, seated at one end of my grandfather's bench. (He was a coat maker and worked for my father, who was a Fifth Avenue tailor.) I would sit at his bench reading one of my books. Sometimes I read to him aloud. Sometimes he handed me a couple of pieces of cloth, a needle and thread, and told me to make something to please my father when he would come home. (Even at that early date there was a conspiracy afoot to make me a tailor too.)

Sometimes I brought Stanley (my first friend) to the room that grandfather worked in. We would play with my toys while my grandfather sang "Shoo-fly, don't bother me. . ."—his favorite ditty.

In that same room, on a rainy day, I recall singing songs in a hearty, lusty voice. And my aunt, working in the kitchen nearby, would come out and clap her hands, kiss me, beg me to sing some more.

Years later, many years later, with Val or Tony on my back, I would trudge through the forest teaching them songs like "Yankee

Doodle Dandy" and the like. They loved these jaunts through the forest.

One of the outstanding things about this period, which is so vivid in my memory, is that already we were incipient psychologists. We (Stanley and I) had every boy in the neighborhood sized up. The heroes, like Eddie Carney and Lester Reardon, stood apart. When Lester Reardon walked down North First Street—just one block—I stood in awe, watching him. If he had been the Pope, I could not have paid more reverence. Then there were the potential criminals, like Alfie Letcha and Johnny Goeller. As a matter of fact, they both ended up in Sing Sing.

Sing Sing! A notorious prison on the Hudson. One day, again many years later, the ex-warden of Sing Sing comes to visit me at my office in the Western Union Telegraph Co., where I was then employment manager. He came, representing some Catholic organization which tried to rehabilitate ex-convicts. I told him immediately that I was forbidden to hire ex-convicts. He disregarded my remark and began telling me he would pay with his life for any misdemeanor on the part of anyone he sent me. I was so taken by his earnestness that I hired three or four ex-convicts the next day. Not only did I find them efficient and reliable (which the young boys were not!) but, on leaving the service they would always come to thank me for what I had done and leave me some token gifts, such as a ring or a watch. Often they blessed me. . . .

UNCLE HARRY

In several of my books I have dwelled on ancestral stock, usually playing up the Germanic strain. At bottom, to be sure, I look upon the German blood as of fairly recent origin. We all know how Europe was ravished again and again by alien hordes. In a word the real German, real Frenchman, real Spaniard, etc., etc. is rare indeed. All Europeans are of mixed blood. Even America is nothing but a mixture of very different races—the only true

American being the despised, the outcast Indian. To conclude this brief preamble, myself I disavow my supposed heritage, and trace it back to very early times. Thereby concluding, in my own mind, that I am a mixture of Mongol, Chinese, Tibetan, and Jewish bloods. . . . And now for the other side of the picture— the homespun dour East American, so to say.

Uncle Harry. With Uncle Harry a wholly new blood strain crept into the Miller-Nieting family. Harry was born Harry Smith of an up-N.Y. State old American family. But he first appeared on the scene at 662 Driggs Ave., under the name of Harry Brown. That was because he was courting Aunt Mary, my favorite aunt of the Nieting tribe. She was eighteen or twenty years old at the time and I just a tot of six or seven. Harry Brown came bouncing into our quiet family life, with buck teeth and a boozy breath. My grandfather, father of Aunt Mary, looked upon Harry Brown immediately as a no-good sort of bum. But my Aunt seemed stuck on him and so Harry lingered on and around.

Then one day it was discovered that he was masquerading under a false name, that his real name was Smith, not Brown. This caused quite a commotion for a while. If I remember rightly, it ended by Harry bringing his mother and his Aunt Joy down from Newburgh to show that he was of decent stock and not an ex-convict or something of the sort.

Grandma Smith, as we called his mother (why I don't know), was a very personable woman. She was about 60 years old, same as Grandpa Nieting, and, oddly enough, those two very different creatures soon got to like one another very much. As a boy, I remember what a thrill it gave me to hear Grandma Smith address Grandpa as "my dear Mr. Nieting." Her voice was lovely, charming, soothing, so different from the voices of the Nieting family. We soon learned that *her* ancestors had come over on the Mayflower.

Naturally, Harry was quickly absolved of his pecadillos. But that was only his first mistake—Brown—Smith. Soon he was accused of rifling the petty cash in the office where he worked. And, after that came the discovery that he was a booze hound. (Had they looked a little deeper they would have uncovered that he was a cunt-chaser too.) With it all Harry was a good fellow, full of cheer, always alert and bright, always with another scheme up his sleeve—all these elements new and disturbing to the Miller-Nieting ménage.

When there was a family reunion, entailing endless cooking, decorations, speeches, and what not, I and my little cousins would be obliged to make frequent visits to the side door of the saloon across the street and bring back huge pitchers of foaming lager. One of Harry's most distinguished traits was his smile. In those days it was referred to as the smile that won't come off. One died with that sort of smile on one's lips.

Often, during a long day of festivities, the uncles would go out "for a walk," as they put it. Actually, it was to do a bit of private pub crawling. There were two famous saloons in our neighborhood. The one across the street from our house and the other at the corner of Grand St. It was this latter saloon, owned and run by the ward healer Pat McCarren, that our uncles loved to patronize. Pat McCarren was often there himself, spouting away, and always in a frock coat with a shamrock in the buttonhole. He wore a stovepipe hat which lent him a solemn air. He was indeed from "the ould country."

Anyway, whenever we kids were ordered to scout for our uncles and bring them home for dinner, we would always repair first to Pat McCarren's saloon. We would first kneel in the doorway and look under the swinging doors. Sure enough, there would be Harry at the bar with a tall glass of beer in his hand, a sailor straw hat cocked to one side, his moustache full of foam and delivering his opinions about this and that while the others tackled the free lunch. Smiling as usual, of course.

Harry was at his best at funerals. It was customary after the burial for the family and relations to go to the beer garden just opposite the cemetery gates—"Trommer's" it was called—and regale themselves with food and drink. During these feasts anecdotes were exchanged about the deceased. Always with a humorous or ridiculous touch. Harry was a master at this. It was right up his street. He could mock and mimic the deceased to a T.

When his own little son died, a boy just a year or two younger than myself, his mother—good old Aunt Mary—decided to hold funeral services at their own home. She invited the minister of their church to do the ritual. I was seated up front, I remember, and had a hard time keeping a straight face, because on solemn occasions I always had nervous fits of laughter. The minister was handing out the usual shit about how our little angel was now safely in Heaven. I was as red as a beet from restraining my laughter. Suddenly out of the corner of my eye I caught Uncle Harry tiptoeing into the kitchen. I knew what he went there for— to down a quick bottle of beer. Soon he returned and the minister droned on. Harry repeated the performance several times, until finally the minister realized something was amiss. He threw a disconcerted glance at my Aunt Mary who was already suspicious of her husband's behavior. Suddenly she followed Harry into the kitchen and soon I heard her grieved, upraised voice exclaiming: "Oh Harry, not now, not *here*. How could you? And Howard (the dead son) lying in the next room. And the minister delivering such a beautiful funeral oration. . . ." Etc., etc. After which Harry stole back to his seat with a grin from ear to ear. When the minister left he addressed the assembled relatives and neighbors now with a broad unashamed smile: "Friends," he began, "nobody could love little Howard more than I. The minister told you he was safely in Heaven. That got my goat. That's why I had to have a drink and another and another." His grin had broadened into an outrageous, sacrilegious smile. "You all know," he continued, "that I was never much for church. I never believed in Heaven or Hell nor angels and devils either. (By now Aunt Mary was sobbing hysterically.)

"Maybe what I did the minister calls a *sin*. I don't know much about sin either. I always do pretty much as I please, whether the minister likes it or not."

(By now the room was almost empty. And I can see my own mother with one hand over her mouth in hypocritical fashion as usual.)

In short, Harry never finished the speech. But I never forgot his words or his attitude. Even at that tender age I didn't have any use for fucking and fucked up ministers of the clergy.

Harry died a happy death—in the mud gutter during a prolonged spree. His straw hat was lying beside him. There was a broad smile on his face.

BONNIE AND CLYDE:
A TOCCATA FOR HALF-WITS

I had intended to sit down and let loose a stream of vitriol the morning after I saw the film, which is now three weeks ago, alas, and in the meantime I have cooled off somewhat. Nevertheless I am still furious, more toward the public which acclaims it *and enjoys it* than toward the producer and director, though I hold them fully responsible for this monstrous piece of entertainment.

I had never thought of seeing the film, after learning of the subject matter, until some of my good friends whose opinion I value urged me not to miss it. And so, taking three friends with me, I finally went to see it. In the first ten minutes I was ready to walk out. I was thoroughly bored, not to say disgusted by the sheer idiocy of the film. I waited for the supposed hilarity, for the sensational riot of fun. Only once during the entire showing did I crack a smile: I never once laughed, nor did I hear any hearty laughter from the audience, only an occasional titter.

I thought I was prepared for all the killing that goes on, having been told that it was all "innocent," "accidental," and so on, and that Bonnie and Clyde were a jolly, lovable pair who never intended to commit all the crimes which they did. But from the first murder till the last, try as I might, I got no fun out of it, only more and more disgust. I might say parenthetically that, like most American movie goers and TV victims, I have absorbed extraordinary doses of murder, rape, torture, and brutality unimaginable in my time. I remember once, when my son was about eight or nine, asking him why he always turned on these gruesome films and his reply was: "But little boys like murder once in a while!" I should add right here that I am not against, or rather I can understand, killing in self-defense or in a moment of blind passion; if I were a judge I would find it difficult to condemn such an act, since in this respect we are all potential killers. But wanton, senseless killing, cold-blooded murder, is another matter. Certainly murderers as a whole are sick people and should be treated as such rather than as criminals.

But what is worse than cold-blooded murder, in my opinion, is the presentation of murder as a form of entertainment. In such instances I feel compelled to look upon the viewers as even more sick than the killers they are watching. As regards the men who make money from such productions, I consider them not only as sick but as evil-minded individuals. They *know* what they are doing, they are not unintelligent. Yet they seem to lack all sense of guilt. They not only seek profit for their labors but fame and glory.

Curiously enough, the one film in this category which is an exception is Chaplin's *Monsieur Verdoux*. It was taken out of circulation before it had run very long, not so much because of the subject matter but because at the time it came out Chaplin was not in good odor in this country. This film, contrary to *Bonnie & Clyde*, was not only one of the funniest pictures I have ever seen but it also pointed a moral. Now would be an opportune moment to revive it. Now the moral of the tale is more likely to be appreciated, if not by the censors, then by the general public. For now we are in the midst of a senseless war[1] when once again all values have been upset, and right and wrong are more than ever confounded. Compared to what the military are doing, and what they are prepared to do in the face of so-called necessity, the murders perpetuated by a Bluebeard seem like child's play. Moreover, Chaplin's Bluebeard, alias Monsieur Verdoux, is not a psychopath but an intelligent human being much like you or I.

Today it is virtually taken for granted that ours is a sick society. Not only do statistics prove it but our leaders themselves proclaim it from the rooftops. Though I have been against our way of life ever since I was a young man, I have now covered a span of life sufficient to make vivid comparison between this period and the one I knew when I was a young man. With my own eyes I have

[1] Vietnam War. This piece written at that time.

witnessed what Whitman wrote of a hundred years ago, namely, the steady deterioration of the individual, the ever increasing corruption from the lowest to the highest levels of society, the increased resort to violence, frequently just for kicks, and the growing frenzy of senseless activity which can only be likened to some form of insanity. Whitman was not a Communist any more than Thoreau, Emerson, or other outspoken American writers. They were more American, indeed, than those who maligned and vilified them. They were seers, and like the prophets of old, they exposed the weaknesses of our people and the seeds of decay. As Georges Duhamel put it in one of his books: "America is like a fruit that rots before it has ripened."

What was not so marked in Whitman's time, it seems to me, is the frightening proportion of morons, imbeciles, psychopaths, and schizophrenics in our population. The number of mentally sick and criminal-minded in our midst today is absolutely alarming. We find them in all classes of society, and not just among the poor and down-trodden. We find them among our Congressmen as well as among our teachers, preachers, and do-gooders, especially among our do-gooders. Gradually we are discovering that what makes for success does not make for a healthy society. The Hippies may be goofy, unsocial, even drug addicts, but they have the good sense to reject current values, to remain apart, to make merry while Rome burns. Maybe they are not as crazy as we would like to believe. Maybe there is an element of a new sanity in their weird behavior. Maybe by refusing to be the Gadarene swine which most of us are they are injecting an element of hope and courage into our confused, frustrated, and desperate society.

And what has all this to do with *Bonnie and Clyde*? Everything. Bonnie and Clyde are morons, and so is C.W., whom I confess I feel more sympathetic toward than the others in the film. Bonnie and Clyde are sick, sick to the core. They smell bad. There is an aura of perversion about them, as well as stupid viciousness. In the case of the real Bonnie and Clyde I am given to understand that Clyde was a homosexual and Bonnie a sort of swinger who "did her thing," as they say, with no matter whom. She was supposed to be doing it with their companion, C.W. But in the film version Clyde is made out to be impotent and Bonnie some sort of half-witted sex maniac who stays slap happy no matter what gives.

One of the first things which turned me off, in the film, was the kind of half-witted way in which the two get together. There is Clyde, with a hebephrenic grin half sex half idiot, and Bonnie, all sex and no brains—like two lollypops saying Hello. The dialogue is nil, as it remains throughout the film. Then comes the scene in the car, with Bonnie devouring Clyde, hungry bitch that she is, and Clyde reacting like a castrated knight of the Round Table. Immediately one senses that something is rotten in Denmark. Immediately one senses that violence is the thing, not love, not sex. The impotent man with the gat gets his kick with the kill, not with his penis. Sick, sick.

And then the humor, such as it is. Somehow, though I have met the hillbillies, the tar heels, and the crackers, though I've travelled the backward regions of the South, I can't dig what passes for humor between Clyde and his brother, or between Clyde, Bonnie, and any of the other morons. It simply ain't real. No more than the shootings between the killers and the police. All this is fake realism, phony sociological hogwash. Don't insult the Oakies or the Arkies—they're far better than that, far more intelligent, far more sensitive, far more humorous.

And then there's the Grant Wood scene with the mother. The one touch of reality and gravity, but marred by the too obvious Grant Wood simulacrum. Even, toward the end, when the pair wish for a better life, for a way out, for what one might call "a decent way of life," it doesn't ring true. Two such half-wits haven't got it in them to know what a better way of life might be. What could a guy like Clyde do, for example? He has no brains, no feelings, no nothing. As for Bonnie, the only thing I could expect her to do is to make a first rate whore, a real whore—*but can she?* She's too fucked up to make anything or to be anything. She was a lost soul from the start. She was headed nowhere and she got nowhere. Frankly, though it goes against my principles to say it, the best moment in the film for me was when the two are finally riddled with bullets in the car. It seemed like a just and merciful end to their cavortings. They lie there like so much human garbage. They served no purpose in life, they had no possible future, and, one surmises, even in Hell they will be misfits.

CADENZA

The other day I saw a new film advertised; the caption read "Even more violent than *Bonnie & Clyde.*" I also read in the papers of a young couple trying to imitate Bonnie and Clyde; unfortunately I don't remember how many they had killed before being apprehended. There will certainly be more imitators as time goes on and the film penetrates the hinterland.

What is sorely needed now as an antidote is a rash of erotic, pornographic, or obscene films, the more censorable the better. If the Hippies are on the love kick, what their elders need is the sex kick. Now and then, to be sure, we get such films from Sweden, Denmark, and other small countries whose inhabitants are well fed, immune to shock treatment, ultra normal, and in general bored to death. But what we need are American films of this variety. What we usually get from Hollywood are teasers; we never go the whole hog, as we are now doing in literature.

Anyway, what a relief it would be to see some real warm-hearted fucking on the screen. Relaxing, to say the least. I mean honest to God intercourse, not spiced with perversion, brutality, and dementia praecox. If any condiments were needed, why not a bit of froth and foam from Billy Graham, or an ecumenical epiphany from the Pope, or a Molotov cocktail à la Phyllis Diller? In other words reality instead of realism, instinct versus abstraction. How really strange, when you thing of it, that you can sell people violence and perversity but not healthy, joyous sexual intercourse! If it is permissible in gangster and spy films, for example, to show victims being kicked in the face or in the balls, to show young punks slashing one another with knives or setting someone aflame with gasoline, or a sniper picking an innocent driver off with a shot gun, why is it not permissible to show the sexual organs engaged in friendly combat?

I say nothing of documentary films in which we see the enemy being routed out of caves with flame throwers, or smoked out with phosphorus, or burned to a crisp with Napalm, or torn to shreds with fragmentation or guava bombs, et cetera et cetera. Such films aren't offered to the public for entertainment but for instruction. They want us to know that "war is hell," but that war is necessary every ten or twenty years, otherwise civilization condones mass slaughter, destruction of the soil and all means of subsistence, condones destruction of churches, libraries, museums, hospitals. . . . What does it not condone in the holy name of civilization? Peace, how wonderful! But peace, oddly enough, is always something that has to be fought for. Peace comes only as the kiss of death.

Just as the movie makers seem to feel that no one will go to the movies if there is not sensationalism and violence, so governments, the big ones, at least, seem to think that people will get too comfortable, too peaceful, too smug and content, if there are no wars.

And does all this have anything to do with *Bonnie & Clyde?* Yes, in the sense that a people which finds senseless murder funny and entertaining can hardly be shocked when they find themselves in the midst of war. How noticeable it is, when listening to the news reports which are largely filled with murder, rape, and arson, if not corruption, mendacity, and treachery in high places, how monstrous and obscene it is to watch commercials about bad breath, headaches, and other disorders following upon the assassination of an important figure or the destruction of a whole village by earthquake or volcano. The cosmetic, the depilatory, the silky toilet paper get almost equal space and attention as the horripilating disasters. Or take the news commentator himself and his manner of reporting the varied happenings of the day. Does he ever break down with grief, does he ever become paralyzed by the horror and gravity of his reports? He goes from horrendous, nauseating, shocking incidents to the trivia of everyday life with scarcely a change of intonation in his voice. He avoids comment of his own, even though the news is shattering. He likens himself as much as possible to a machine, a tape recorder, a tickertape. Even the reporters at the front try as much as possible to keep their *sang-froid*. We want facts, not emotions, sensation but no hang-overs.

And despite all the cold-blooded accounting and recounting, the facts are often lies. It depends on who is reporting, on who is putting up the dough, on who is trying to save face, or whose pocket is being hurt. We can't depend on governments for the truth nor upon reporters whose hands are tied and mouths gagged. We can't even depend on our own intelligence and acumen, for we are all brain-washed and walking in our sleep.

As the Zulus say—"The time of the hyena is upon us." The Brazilians put it another way: "When shit acquires value the poor are born without ass-holes." And if I may add my own little bit, I would say: "What we thrive on is hatred and violence; if we were a peaceable people we would have peace tomorrow."

And so, to be downright honest, we must conclude (editorially speaking) that the real monsters are not Bonnie and Clyde but we, the public at large. We sit back in our comfortable seats, our bread baskets stuffed with rich food, and we say—"Sock it to us, we'll take anything you've got." We pay without slightest complaint to be shocked, nauseated, terrified, and brain-washed. And on the day of atonement, when the awards are handed out, the men who served these ugly dishes are given the Oscar. What could be fairer? So, Mr. Beatty, Miss Dunaway, Mr. Penn, Mr. Newman and Mr. Benton, Mr. Warner Bros., if I appear to have been a little harsh, a little too broad and sweeping in my criticism of your creation, please know that in the last analysis your *Bonnie & Clyde* is but a tiny symbol of all that ails us, and that in my heart of hearts I don't think you are really any worse than many other members of your clan. In fact, I am almost certain that, given a bit of pot or a dose of L.S.D., you may come up one day with something really funny, really entertaining, if not instructive or therapeutic.

Dear Irv!

Answering your Yom Kippur letter only now. Still without new glasses. I sent that letter (order) from Irishman to Noel Young. *Joey* just out. Got only (1) copy but ordered twenty-five or more. Will have one for you shortly. (Looks great!) Tagore was and still is great favorite of mine. (Know his *My Religion*?) Calcutta (in the muck) is a great city for artists. Remember his School— "Shantiniketan"?

(Do you want *to be cured* of A.?) Strikes me strange.

Sava now putting ad in L.A. *Times Book Review*. I'm sure they'll sell out. Did a "Conversation" with Barbara Kraft for National Public Radio. And one with Evelyn Hinz for Lawrence Festival in Taos next July. Also my book (*World of Lawrence*) coming out before too long. Noel thinks it best thing I've done so far (sic!).

Never heard of Nishi or Mishi![1] Will ask patron at Imperial Gardens, if I remember!

Zacharius *seems* like a very good guy to me. Spent an afternoon here. May publish three books dropped by NAL two years ago.

Irv—I've wanted to make *you* a gift of a Munakata[2] album for long time. Trouble is, don't know publisher's name & address. Always given only in Japanese.

But look, I received a free copy from Japanese Playboy mag. They have an office in N.Y. City. Could you ask them if they know where to order, the price, etc. Say it's for *me*, that I am crazy about his work! And ask for an album that has the most *color* reproductions. That way I may yet get book for you! He'll

---

[1] A Japanese word whose exact meaning puzzled correspondent Irv Stettner.
[2] Shikō Munakata, renowned Japanese artist.

drive you nuts, I'm sure. I try to paint like him now, when I do paint. If only I had another pair of eyes!

Cheerio!

Henry

That watercolor you so generously gave C. Nazareth is greatest of yours I have seen so far. An absolute beauty! And what draught-manship! *Incroyable!* I wanted to dance!

WATER COLOR 1979 / HENRY MILLER

AMERICA, AMERICA*

Europeans of mixed heritage set out to see as much of America as their limited means would permit. Instead of a book about their experiences they tell their story with photos.

Did they have preconceived notions about this country of ours? Probably, who wouldn't? Doesn't the whole world know about America? Do *Americans* know their America, that is the question. From my own experience in dealing with my compatriots I would say no, or very poorly. How many have left their native route or even city? It costs money to travel today and most Americans, supposedly so well off, cannot afford to do it. Another legitimate question would be—do they *care* to know their own country? As everyone is well aware, it is dangerous to travel about in the big cities.

The men who composed this book made it a point to see both cities and countryside. They naturally photographed the high-and-low lights of such places as New York, New Orleans, San Francisco, Chicago, Los Angeles, Las Vegas, to name a few. But they also explored the vast open spaces of Arizona, Nevada, Utah, and Colorado.

What we have therefore are two different Americas; the one that man has made and which is falling apart and the one God made, apparently to outlast man. The grandiose places which belong to nature, such as the Grand Canyon, the Rocky Mountains, the Great Smokies still defy man's devilry. The hillbillies of the deep South have not lost their warmth, their hospitality, their carefree nature. The Blacks and the Mexicans play a predominant role in our life. The American Indian is still an exile in his own land, the land we robbed him of. When we say American consequently we mean many different kinds of creatures.

* Note: Henry Miller wrote this essay for Michel Waxman and André Cromphont as a foreword for a book of photographs to be published by Editions Complete, Brussels, Belgium.

Most Americans would appear to be immigrants. Many, many Americans are uneducated, poverty-stricken, desperate. And in the midst of all the chaos and the confusion we find that strange gazebo called the politician. He is our friend and enemy at the same time. But he belongs to another order of nature.

This book might well be entitled "Man Versus Nature." Despite all man's efforts to defile nature he still remains as puny and ineffective as a bed bug. He is a threat rather than a curse. It is he who has created the cities, most of them modern infernos. And yet, as one will observe in some of these photos—notably of the South Bronx, N.Y.—the Black people of the ghettos can still laugh, a laugh which the white man has never learned. He can also make music out of his misery: it may not be "classic" music, but it is music. Perhaps *soul music* would be the appropriate definition. Indeed, despite the high percentage of crimes attributed to him he still has a soul. (The white man lost his ages ago, no matter what Billy Graham may say.)

Speaking of the deprived and the down-trodden I must put in a word for the hillbillies and other so-called backward peoples scattered throughout the land, often indeed occupying the most beautiful regions of this great country. Whereas tourists and natives alike are warned to be on guard when traveling about the cities, the supposedly "inferior" people who are joked about and made to look ridiculous are warm, friendly, hospitable. *And* they care for the regions they grew up in. They preserve and conserve in contrast to the destructive tendencies of the supposedly "superior" class.

There are towns and villages which 90% of the population never heard of; one is Biloxi, Mississippi, which I made a point to visit on my *Air-conditioned Nightmare* trip. Let me add that from all reports it is just as beautiful today as forty or fifty years ago.

How few places in these States can one say that of? Wherever the American passes he leaves behind a wasteland.

Fortunately, our two foreigners made the effort to see God's handiwork. One hears a great deal about Europe and Asia, the marvels there to behold, but in the Western States and much of the South (the old South) there is beauty unsurpassed. Beauty and grandeur. And that is what is so surprising about the average American—that so little of this beauty and grandeur has rubbed off on him.

I gave the title of my Preface the same title as the famous film by Elia Kazan. Despite all the misery which is rampant in our country the eyes of the poor foreigner are still on this country. It does not take long for them to be disillusioned. Oddly enough it is this same foreigner who is the backbone of America. We are all foreigners at bottom; all but the Indians who we have never treated decently. He too, like the hillbilly inhabits some of the most scenic parts of America. An interesting fact again is that these wonderful parts of America have a very low economic yield. God evidently was not interested in money-making.

I have spoken of the slums and ghettos of our country. Yet for the style of life practiced by a good portion of the white population they might just as well be living in the slums and ghettos. Their slums and ghettos are of the mind—probably worse than the real slums and ghettos. The professional classes, for example, are as prone to drugs and alcohol as any other portion of the population.

I have not mentioned the real villian, the television set. This hypnotic form of idiocy really has the country by the balls. Our television, or the fare offered, is both the best and the worst. Anything for a buck, as the saying goes. And it is in front of these sets that our youth receives its real education. Over a hundred years ago, our greatest American writer Walt Whitman declared that we were well on our way to becoming a nation of lunatics. We are no longer *becoming*—we are there, loony as bed bugs, destructive as lice and vermin, knowing neither peace, repose, or contentment.

August 25, 1978

Cher Irv—

That was a fantastic letter about the French woman. How much is a lifetime subscription to *Stroker*? Very curious.

Listen. I found out what's wrong with me! First thru Sydney Omarr, the astrologer. Confirmed by my doctor. I have hypolucemia. Must not eat regular meals—only snacks (full of protein), sugar the big enemy. Have no wine, no strawberry yogurt, only natural yogurt, slivers of cheese now and then. Strange but tried eating just a bowl of (wrong) yogurt last night at dinner—with green tea and felt fine. But then I had good company—my twenty-three year old (genius) friend from Chile—Einar Moos. A fantastic bird. Most interesting person in my entourage.

I too have made eight or nine W'C'S recently—and like them immensely. Bill Pickerill hopes to make fair sized photos of them—then I can give you idea of what Munakata has done to and for me.

The pkg. from Brentano's must be the Kandinsky book. Hope so! Still letting Sandy handle all my c/s. What a relief! Ooof! But I sure read your letters. You know, it's evident that God is *with* *you*—not on your side. You're being looked after. I told you once *Stroker* will be heard from.

Anyway, you're a Scorpio—like Val, Brenda, et alia.

All the best!

Henry

P.s. It will happen with the coming of Uranus which brings pleasant and *un*pleasant surprises. Haven't had chance to get your horoscope done yet, but can visualize it in my mind.

PPs. Christine Nazareth is nuts about you. Off to Cannes (France) now but back in month or two and will look you up immediately.

Dear Irv—

This flyer just came. It is not quite true that my Ms. on Lawrence was the beginning of this book. In fact, I refused to write a brief work on D.H.L. A few months later, in Clichy, the idea came to do a big work on him. I *suffered* the pangs and onslaughts of "inspiration"—for the first and only time. The book was virtually dictated to me by the "guy upstairs" or some one on that order.

That batch of letters you returned we sent to Noel Young. Please do likewise with succeeding ones. Very very glad to hear of your progress with the Japanese book.[1] That should be a *Loulou* of a book.

Faites *comme vous voudrez*!

Cheers!
Henry

Made some more water colors last few days. I like them! Good luck with your'n!

---

[1] *Chocolate Soldier in Tokyo*

A FEW COMPASSIONATE WORDS
FOR BROTHER BILL

For Brother Bill Pickerill[1] of the Order of Cappadocian monks a few words of compassion and nutriment to a fellow sinner. This is your time, your place, your opportunity. Make the most of it; squeeze all the color out of the tubes. Dance the dance of the seven veils. Make merry desperately. There only comes this one time—to us an eternity, to the gods a passing shadow. Make believe your studio gives out on the Riviera. There really ain't any such place except in the head. Have a good headache cum baccalaureate!

Brother Henry
2/7/80

---

[1] A young American painter.

New Directions Paperbooks—A Partial Listing

For complete listing request free catalog from
New Directions, 80 Eighth Avenue, New York 10011

†Bilingu

For complete listing request free catalog from
New Directions, 80 Eighth Avenue, New York 10011   †Bilingual